Liar, Liar

Expose Lies, Discover Truth, Experience Healing

Thomas L. Hall

Liar, Liar
Expose Lies, Discover Truth, Experience Healing

Copyright © 2018 by Thomas L. Hall
ISBN: 978-0998101385

Empyrion Publishing
PO Box 784327
Winter Garden, FL
info@EmpyrionPublishing.com

Unless otherwise notated, all Scripture quotations are from the King James Version of the Bible.

New King James is notated as NKJV
English Standard Version is notated as ESV
New International Version is notated as NIV
The Bible in Basic English is notated as BBE

Cover design by Matthew T. Hall

Printed in the United States of America

Dedication

I am grateful to dedicate this book to those ministers who gave great portions of their lives to my development: Rev. Emma Cammuse, Rev. Charles McKinley, Rev. Ken Greene, Rev. R.G. and Phyllis Roberts (who are still my pastors today); and Rev. Gary Clowers who, as a prophetic voice, has helped to unveil God's plans for my life.

I dedicate this book to the faithful men and women, teachers, group leaders, pastoral team and friends from The Church of the Living God in Winchester, Kentucky. Thank you for twenty-six years of partnership, and counting!

Most of all, I dedicate this book to my family. Lela, my wife and partner, the greatest mother and grand-mommy: you are the glue to our lineage. Matthew and Heather, Meagan and John, Kiana: your mother and I are humbled by your love for us, how you labor beside us, leading COLG to impact many, many lives here and around the world. To our precious granddaughters, Keeley, Natalie, Maddy, and Evie: you are our legacy in a new generation.

Table of Contents

Introduction

It was May 1972 in the afternoon session of a multi-church youth rally being hosted by the Pentecostal Church of God in Lawrenceburg, Kentucky. The morning session was powerfully preached by the state youth director, Reverend R.G. Roberts. As the afternoon session began, my thoughts drifted back to the last rally, in April, when it was announced that any young people who "felt a call to preach" were invited to do so during the afternoon session in May.

Between the April and May services, just about all I could think about was what I would preach when it was my time to take the pulpit. Suddenly, my name was called, jolting me back to the present. I stepped out of my seat, into the aisle, and headed toward the platform.

When I arrived, the leadership determined I could not stand behind the pulpit because it was taller than I was! From the back of the room, someone brought a suitable item for me to stand on, and from there, I preached my very first sermon to a congregation. I was nine years old. It was not a memorable message, yet I cannot forget that day of beginnings.

Action Must Follow Purpose

For I know the thoughts that I think toward you, saith the Lord, thoughts of peace, and not of evil, to give you an expected end.

Then shall ye call upon me, and ye shall go and pray unto me, and I will hearken unto you.

And ye shall seek me, and find me, when ye shall search for me with all your heart. (Jer. 29:11-13)

The statement, "To give you an expected end" suggests the thoughts and purposes of God about our lives are not idle or momentary. His thoughts are not simply about our past and present; they are reaching into the very end of our lives.

Jeremiah 29:11 is somewhat famous. We see it on Bible covers, posters and t-shirts. However, to receive the full impact of what Prophet Jeremiah is saying, we must continue to read Jeremiah 29:12-13 as well.

As God's thoughts are of peace and not evil, and He has promised to give us an expected end, can't we just lean back in the recliner or stretch out on the couch, waiting for God's plan to arrive? Not yet, if we are to consider Jeremiah 29:12, "Then shall ye call upon me."

This revelation is not meant to shift our gears into cruise control while we wait for God to arrange the arrival of our expected end. This revelation is not even purposed to move us to seek "the plan of God" but instead to seek *the God* who has the plan!

> Then shall ye call upon *me*, and ye shall go and pray unto *me*, and I will hearken unto you. And ye shall seek *me*, and find *me*, when ye shall search for *me* with all your heart. (Jeremiah 29:12-13, *emphasis mine*)

The very truth that there is a purpose for our lives should stimulate us beyond a routine prayer life and into the life of a persistent seeker of God Himself. One way to do this is to agree with God that He has a purpose for you. Confess your belief that you are not a cosmic accident and accept you are here with eternal purpose. Beyond this, it is not difficult to seek God.

As a persistent seeker of God, tell Him you are seeking Him, tell Him you are seeking His will – then do it. Call upon Him, pray unto Him, seek Him, then find Him. When you search for God with all your heart, then you will find Him. His promise is not for His gain, but for ours. As we witness God hearkening unto us, we are ready to seek and find God. After all, if He is willingly imperfect in anything, it is in hiding.

As our prayer life matures toward the direction of persistently searching for the plan of God with all our heart, we begin to discover that He is not hiding, let alone lost. It is we who hide, as Adam did in the Garden of Eden. Like Adam, we are hiding from ourselves. Therefore, we understand to find God is to find our purpose. In 1972, I committed my life to discovering God's purpose for this plumber's kid from Salvisa, Kentucky.

God has many ways of leading us toward our future. He confirmed to my leaders there was a call on my life. As I sought God's purpose for me, these mentors and coaches became encouragers and instructors to my life. God will use people with similar callings to reinforce to us that they also can discern this calling.

In 1979 at sixteen years old, another significant happening in my young life was a prophetic word I received from a guest preacher who came to our church for revival. The wonderful man of God who spoke this powerful message of destiny confessed years later he almost held it back because I was so young. In fact, he claims I only looked twelve years old. He has remained a voice in my life and ministry ever since.

Here is that message:

"The young man with his hands in the air in the back, there's a ministry in your life, Whether you know it or not, there is a ministry in your life. God has asked me to speak to you tonight, and I'm going to tell you one thing, young man – the hand of God is upon you. You will not ever, *ever* be able to live as one of those who fit into the puzzle. You are always going to be a puzzle piece that seemingly does not fit, and you know why? Because the calling of God is upon you, and I'm going to tell you right now, son, there's a ministry shut up in your bosom they haven't heard yet.

God said there's an anointing shut up within you they haven't seen yet, and they won't see for a while, but God said you have knowledge already of what I'm speaking to you tonight – that the ministry is shut up within you. You know there was a scripture where Jeremiah said it is, "a burning fire shut up in my bones," (Jer. 20:9) and that's just simply the way it is! I'm going to tell you right now there is a phenomenon that's going to take place and you're going to be able to make manifest the blessings of God.

God is going to use you at an early age and people will be surprised because you are young. But God said, "I will use you at an early age." I don't mean He is going to use you tomorrow, but I do mean at an early age. God said people will be surprised at that which will flow from you because you're gentle. There's love shut up within your heart, within your soul. There's depth in your mind, and God said, "I'm going to open up those caverns and begin to speak knowledge into them, and you're going to reveal what the presence of God has wrought in you."

From those days to these days, I want to share with you some of the experiences and truths God has given to change my life and the lives of many others. To God be the glory, for He is the One who dared to dream a plan for my life.

Let us begin with the fulfillment of the phenomenon spoken of in this mighty prophecy. It would take me into great heartbreak and sorrow, revealing my own insecurities, doubts and fears as I journeyed from earth to heaven, standing in the courtroom of God, and back again.

1

Courtroom of God

It was ten days before my 31st birthday on a Sunday evening, March 6, 1994. We had returned home and settled in after the evening service at the church we pastor. I remember the satisfaction of coming to the end of such a good day as I sat back in my recliner. Our children, Matthew and Meagan, were down for the night and it was getting time for us to call it a day as well.

The peace and quiet was interrupted by the ringing of the phone. My wife, Lela, went to the kitchen to answer and I came out of the recliner to get my coat and shoes. A late evening call to the pastor's house generally meant I was on my way to meet a crisis.

I could hear the tone of the conversation from the living room, so I quickly went into the kitchen. Lela was just hanging up the phone, her face was pale and she slowly began to speak. "It's Erik," she said. "He's been in a major car accident; they had to call a helicopter to airlift him to the University of Kentucky hospital." I too went pale.

My brother, Erik, is the youngest of the six Hall family children, turning eighteen the previous December. A senior in high school at the time, with excellent grades, he had recently met with a Marine Corp recruiter who offered him the opportunity for training as a Marine Corp pilot. According to the recruiter, Erik had the ideal body type for such a role with a 6'4" tall frame and a basketball build. If I remember correctly, Erik had signed his intentions just earlier that week.

Lela's mother, Elizabeth, lived with us in our split-level home. She was on the lower level and had already gone to sleep. Lela quickly went downstairs and woke her, and told her of the accident. Elizabeth came upstairs to be available to our children, should they awaken. After making a couple quick calls to other pastors and leaders in the church, we left urgently for the hospital.

Arriving at the University of Kentucky hospital emergency room in record time, we parked and nearly sprinted towards the entrance where a nurse was waiting. She took one look at us and said, "Hall family?" "Yes," I said, as she led us through a door to the left and into a small family room. This emphasized to me, once again, the urgency of the injuries. We were not sitting in the general seating area waiting to be called. We had our own room, not a good sign.

Two of my sisters and a brother-in-law were already in the room. My father was parking his car. Not long after we arrived, a member of the neurology surgical team came in to give us information concerning the accident.

Erik and two other teenagers were in the front seat of the car, he was driving. Something happened to cause him to run off the road and into one of the fences on a beautiful Central Kentucky horse farm. The other two passengers were virtually uninjured, and Erik had really just one injury. As pieces of fence went flying, coming through the windshield and into the car, one of them, about eight inches long, a couple inches or so thick, hit Erik just above the right eyebrow.

The force was strong enough to break Erik's skull. This foreign object was now lodged into the frontal lobe of his brain, requiring open brain surgery to remove. The doctor informed us the intricate and urgent effort to save his life was currently in progress, would take hours, and was unlikely to succeed. The incision was like a half circle, arching from above his eyebrow back to his right ear to allow for brain tissue to be removed.

They moved us from this small waiting room into a larger one to make us a little more comfortable as we waited through the night. A couple church leaders joined us, as well as Tony, a pastor from another town who played on our church basketball team that year. He had been giving Erik a ride to the games. We were all so very stunned. The night moved very slowly.

The Monday morning light began to break, revealing it was just cold enough overnight to coat the trees with light ice. "A little late in the year for that," I thought, "but somehow fitting."

We were finally updated by a surgical assistant. Erik survived the surgery and was being moved to the Neurosurgery Intensive Care Unit. We were shown to the Neurosurgery ICU waiting room, but were told it would be some time before we could see Erik. He remained in very critical condition. Some who stayed overnight with us left for home and work, while immediate family remained, waiting to see what the day would bring.

Late in the morning, a nurse told us we could see Erik. I took a moment to speak to her, explaining I was Erik's brother and pastor, and I wanted to see him first in order to gain some composure and prepare the rest of the family for what we were going to see as we stepped into the unit. I especially wanted to be strong for my dad when he would first see his youngest in such a condition. I dreaded going back there, but Ray, one of my great friends and a co-worker at church, had arrived and agreed to go back with me. Ray was my father's age and knew Dad from Eastern Kentucky where they grew up. Before we went back to see Erik, the gracious nurse had some information for me. On the top of her clipboard was a sheet filled with images representing the many different kinds of machines possibly in operation to help sustain any patient's life. She looked at the sheet, considering each machine, then drew a circle around the entire page. She told Ray and me they were using, pretty much, everything they had at this point in time to help Erik, including a ventilator assisting Erik in breathing.

We were led to the daunting double doors closest to Erik's bed. As we pushed the doors open, his bed was directly in front of us. We passed three units on our left as we came to the foot of my baby brother's bed. In the weeks to come, this bed would become a great battleground. The space around the top of the bed was filled with machinery, tubes running from all directions. The sounds of beeps and moving machines were an orchestra of activity, playing as background music to the drama unfolding before us.

Erik's bandages began just above his eyebrows and went over his head like a cap. There was a tube at the top of his head for drainage of fluids and to monitor the inter-cranial pressure of his brain. This ICP number would be one of the first things we would look at every time we came back to see him. Erik's physical appearance was deceptively in order. His lips were swollen from the massive amounts of medicines administered during the overnight battle for his life. However, no other broken bones or cuts left him looking much better than I had prepared myself to see.

I couldn't help but think, "If this piece of wood, this stick, had missed him, his biggest concern would have been Dad's reaction to a wrecked car."

The nurse who had been assigned this patient of ours came over to meet us. She was compassionate and professional, taking time to explain all that was flowing into him and what the machines were there to provide or monitor.

She also educated me about the ICP number, a measurement of inter-cranial pressure, which we all have. In our everyday lives, you and I have probably never thought about that number on a day-to-day basis. Honestly, I had never heard of it to this point. As we live and breathe, our ICP number is running at 12 or so. Should something catastrophic occur, the revelation this number reveals is to what extent the brain is swelling. The nurse said we certainly do not want to see this number above 20. Currently, Erik's number was doing okay, with medication.

As the late morning wore into the afternoon, we had the opportunity to go see Erik a couple of family members at a time. There were tears and fears of the unknown. My mother and her husband made it in from Ohio and the wait continued. Phone calls, visiting church members, and seniors from Erik's high school began to come to check on us and him. We learned where the closest cafeteria was, vending machines, and carved out a corner in the waiting room for our bunch.

There were other families there with neurology patients. The waiting room was not only for the neurology ICU, but also burn victims and the very ill. We were numb, tired, and just existing. We really didn't see the other people very much, at first; they seemed like extras on a film site, living in the background. That would change as the weeks went by. We would celebrate with these families when their patients improved and weep with those that did not.

It was late afternoon when we met the actual neurosurgeon who performed the long night's surgery. She was very professional as she explained to us the full extent of the devastating injury the stick, which had invaded Erik's brain, had brought. In fact, "he should have died on impact at the side of the road," she said.

There were many splinters they literally had to do their best to sift out. Much of the frontal right lobe of Erik's brain tissue was removed in that effort.

The doctor said we had two major enemies: one was infection and the other was brain swelling. There are typically three lines of defense against the brain swelling and, unfortunately, they already had to go to the last line, a medication known as pentobarbital. The greatest amount of this medicine they should give was 250 mg. It actually induces a medical coma to keep the brain from 'firing' too much activity, so it can rest and not swell.

Usually, after a head trauma, the 48-72 hour mark becomes a time of life or death. In this window, brain swelling can come on with a vengeance. If that took place we would be in big trouble. The doctor assured us they would continue to maximize efforts to sustain Erik to the best of their ability.

My mother questioned, "Would you give me a ten percent chance my son will survive this accident?"

The reply was, "I'm sorry, I cannot give you that."

"Five percent?" Mom persisted.

"I'm sorry, I cannot give you that."

"Even one percent?" Mom asked desperately.

"I'm sorry, I cannot give you that."

"What then is the prognosis?" Mother asked.

This great doctor simply said, "The prognosis is death," and she walked away.

We were now soaked in the reality that Erik's injury had only one medical outcome, and it was absolutely devastating. I would like to tell you that faith arose, we expressed joy in the middle of sorrow, we stood our ground like an elite fighting team. However, the reality of this prognosis was crushing.

In fact, the first round of mental attacks began to work through the minds of our family. There was a spiritual purpose of the enemy working behind the scenes to bring battles of doubt, fear and accusations, even against God. My mind began to reason this out about the same time my mother was trying to understand as well.

Our conversation went something like this:

"Tommy, why did this happen to Erik?"

"Mom, he lost control of the car, went through a plank fence, and a piece of the plank broke his skull and went into his brain."

"I know that, but why ERIK?" she asked.

"Because, HE lost control of the car, went through a plank fence, and a piece of the plank broke his skull and went into his brain. If anyone else had this accident they would be in the same shape. The natural consequence of his injury is death," was my reply.

We began to wait on through the night into Tuesday morning and on into the afternoon. There was a blur of activity, so much compassion poured out to us from our congregation, our friends in the area, in the state, and even from out of state. So many calls were coming into the hospital they began to give us a list of names from time-to-time. People brought cards, fruit, water and soft drinks. They were doing everything they knew to do, yet the crisis continued to grow.

As Tuesday progressed, the ICP number was increasing. It was now beyond the 20s into the 30s. The amount of pentobarbital medication was also being increased. The evening brought us to the 48-hour mark from the accident. Indeed, the swelling was coming on with a vengeance.

The high school kids were really getting in the way. They forgot where they were, why they were there, and were laughing and playing around, tickling the girls, in and out of the waiting room. Mercifully, they were relocated downstairs to some cafeteria seating. Looking back, I am sure they were not equipped to deal with this scene, and neither were we.

Around 3:00 a.m. Wednesday, my wife and I were downstairs, off to ourselves and I was struggling. I said to her, "Lela, if we were walking down a sidewalk and someone we didn't even know suddenly fell in front of us, wouldn't we pick them up? I mean, if you have the power to help them, isn't it common courtesy to pick them up? I KNOW God has the power to lift Erik, why doesn't HE just reach down and pick him up?"

I was riding the waves of this circumstance. At 31 years-old, I was trying to reconcile an Almighty God, able to do all things, with a dying 18-year-old brother upstairs.

Wednesday daylight did not relieve the concerns. While Erik was still in the fight some very ominous signs began to appear. As the day continued on, Erik's ICP number continued to rise and his feet began to turn inward and cold. Several family members, including my father, mentioned Erik seemed "empty"; "no one at home" when they were back with him. We all wanted to be there for each other, and Erik, if the worst happened.

A friend and fellow pastor, John, had just heard about Erik's accident. Several years ago now, this man, just a little younger than I, came to the first church where we pastored and found a calling to ministry. On this day, John stopped by my pastor's house on his way home from college in Ohio, only to find out about this tragic accident.

He came into the waiting room where we were sitting and got caught up on current conditions. John stood and said, "Tom, let's get out of here for a while." We went downstairs, got a soft drink and sat down at a table.

John looked at me and said, "Tom, you need to fight this."

Honestly, that statement did not sit well with me at all. I said, "John, don't come in here on day four and give me something that cheap. You haven't heard the doctor's reports; you haven't seen the progressive deterioration. We've had NO good news from the minute we arrived."

I told him it seemed the natural course was going to prevail on this situation and it didn't look like there was a thing we could do about it. John said something very frustrating to me, yet it found a place in the back of my mind.

"Isn't it true that if the natural consequences had happened, Erik would have died on the side of the road?" John asked. He prayed with me, and we hugged as he went on his way.

By Wednesday evening, the ICP number approached 40, then 50 and above. Skin was swelling behind Erik's left ear from brain tissue seeping through any cavity it could find. His left eye was dilated and fixed. We were told he was not likely going to live through the night and were given the opportunity to go by his bedside to say our good-byes. It was brutal, to say the least. It was all too real, yet somehow so unreal.

Wednesday night turned to very early Thursday morning, when the neurologist came in to give us an update. They were giving Erik a gram dosage of the pentobarbital, hourly, through the night. He may not even come out of the medically induced coma. The ICP number topped 55 and into the 60s, topping off at 68. It was unthinkable he would have any brain function left. His body was showing signs of brain death: extremities were cold, feet turning in further and now both eyes were dilated and fixed. His pupils were "blown".

The neurologist asked permission to do a nuclear scan to prove the battle was over. The doctor said, "Your family has been here all week, you've done all you can do and so have we. We need to let you good people get on with what you have to do."

We reluctantly agreed and said our good-byes, just before they rolled him to the scan. I chose to say, "See you later" instead of "Good-bye."

My mind was still reasoning, "We are not being picked on, it was an accident. Anyone else would be in this same shape or would have died by the road. The natural consequence of his injuries is death."

We were notified when Erik returned from the scan, the doctor would give us a report later. It turned out to be several hours later when the neurologist came to us. She said, "There's a minimal amount of blood flowing to the brain. It is not enough to sustain him, but it is enough that we legally have to continue to treat him, I'm sorry." She turned and walked away.

I heard clearly what the doctor had to say. I can remember it verbatim, even now. However, there was a stirring inside of me. Deep in my spirit, I began to hear, "There's life in the blood," a reference to Leviticus 17:11. And I heard it over and over.

That night, I was back with Erik by myself and the wonderful nurse assigned to him came over to check on me. The nurses in this unit were really top notch. Sometimes the nurses wore shirts with sayings like, "Neurology department, where miracles happen." These nurses cared immensely and several of them were deeply bothered by what had happened to Erik. A few of the nurses had even asked to be reassigned because of the impact of this circumstance on them. One night a nurse shared just how unfair she felt it was. She said it was always so sad when a young person received mortal wounds from an accident. "This boy wasn't drinking or on drugs while he was driving. Such a sad thing to see a kid like this losing a battle for his life," she said.

As Erik's nurse came near to me, I asked her, "Did you hear about the nuclear scan?" She tilted her head and with a deep expression on her face, she said, "I did Tom, I'm so sorry."

For the first time in this horrible week, faith began to speak out of me. I said, "We are still in this fight; don't be surprised at what may happen here! You may see a light over this bed, or something unexplainable. Many believe as long as there is a chance, a miracle can happen, but I believe even when there is no chance, it's not too late for a miracle."

The nurse patted my hand and gave me a very compassionate look and I could almost hear her thoughts, "He is delusional and refusing to accept the truth." She chose to say, "Tom, once the blood flow restricts, it never increases. Even if it could increase, there are many stroked areas, dead areas of the brain. Once brain cells die, they never rejuvenate." I thanked her for the information, but clung to the thought that we were still in the fight.

Earlier in the day, I told my family we needed to stop grieving Erik. If death came, we could grieve him then, but today was a day of life, it was time to fight.

That night, getting away from our family and friends, I really began to declare some truth brought out of a stirred-up faith. I stood outside of the ICU's double doors where I could see Erik's bed through the crack between them. With my Bible in my hand, I began to speak, "I speak life to Erik Hall; I speak life. I rebuke death off Erik Hall. Death, I rebuke you off of Erik Hall!"

After some time of making this declaration, I was aware I was no longer standing outside of those double doors. In fact, I wasn't in the same place at all. I had entered into a room, standing just inside of two wooden doors. To my right and to my left there were benches for seating. As I pondered this, I saw a light in the front of the room. To say it was bright would be an understatement. It was more than bright; it was the purest light I had ever seen or felt, captivating me.

A man, professional and sharply dressed, stood to his feet in the front, to my left. He shuffled several papers around, then looked toward the light and said exactly this, "Your honor, I make a motion Erik Hall shall die. He is injured beyond what any human being should be able to be healed or to recover from. The natural consequence of his injuries is death." With that, the man took his seat.

For a moment, I considered what had just happened. This man obviously was the "accuser of the brethren", the fallen cherub known as Satan. It amazed me that HE was using MY reasoning in his own motion! Did Satan speak, "The natural consequence of his injuries is death" into my own mind or did he take the statement from my own reasoning and use it in court? Either way, I decided it was the last time I was going to be in agreement with him.

To my right, another man stood, but said nothing. From the pureness of the unforgettable light, a voice spoke. The judge asked, "Is there not anyone here to plead for this boy's life?" The second man turned toward me and extended his left hand. I slowly began to walk toward him, where I arrived at the side of Jesus Christ. He looked to the light and said, "Your honor, my Father, we make a motion for life."

Suddenly, I was back in the hallway of the University Hospital, Bible in hand, knowing God was intervening in Erik's crisis and had now invited me to come into the fight for his life.

Thursday became Friday and physically things were no better. Spiritually, however, things were shifting. As Erik hung in the balance of life and death, I finally agreed to go home for some real rest in my own bed. I slept for around four hours and when I woke up, I cried out to my wife. She came quickly into the room.

"I've had a horrible dream," I told her. "Erik was in a deadly accident, we were all at the hospital. It was a nightmare!"

"I'm so sorry," Lela said. "It wasn't a dream. We will have to get back to the hospital soon." She hugged me and we prepared to go back to Erik's side.

On arrival at the hospital, we learned there had been no changes while we were away. In all earthly reality, Erik's body was in an un-winnable battle. Yet, I knew God was looking for someone to plead for "this boy's life!" We still greeted many people who were there for us; time was either creeping or flying at times. The support we received was humbling and we remain grateful, even now. We would go and stand by Erik's bedside, pat his hand, sometimes pray, other times we shed tears. However, now it seemed as someone was living in that body again!

As visiting hours wound down, things got quieter, and others in the family went home to get some real sleep. I went back to the hallway with Bible in hand. Scriptures began to come into my spirit and I lifted them up to God in prayer.

The approach of prayer had changed greatly. I found myself saying, "Heavenly Father, I have come to call your court into order. I am here to plead for my brother's life." The first scripture used as evidence was Isaiah 53:1. "Who has believed our report? And to whom has the arm of the LORD been revealed?"

Over the weekend I asked God to hear these prayers and to move, to give us a tangible change for the better, a bit of good news. Every prayer session opened with, "I have come to call your court into session. I am here to plead for Erik Hall's life." Scripture was being opened to my spirit and I literally began to pray them back to God. These powerful truths God began to reveal to me brought life into my spirit and mind. I began to understand all He wanted was for me to agree with his Word and heart so He might be able to do that which was already in his heart to do.

On Monday morning, the report came from the doctors that Erik's right eye was no longer dilated and fixed. The brain swelling had subsided some and Erik was still breathing. It was the first bit of good news we received and we were grateful and ready to fight on. Erik's ICP number was also confirming the swelling was lessening. We were still under the prognosis the brain damage was irreversible and life was still hanging in the balance. However, I had asked for good news and it had come.

The doctors discussed doing a tracheotomy because Erik would need the ventilator for permanent breathing assistance. Later in the day, the news arrived that the left eye was also no longer dilated and fixed. The pentobarbital was continually in use, yet the dosage was reduced. There were some ups and downs; in one of the procedures the doctors inadvertently punctured one of his lungs. It caused a few rougher days, but turned out not to be detrimental.

Day after day, eight times, ten times, maybe more, I cried out to God, "I've come to call your court into session; I am here to plead for my brother's life." I was bombarding heaven with scripture I thought I was using to persuade God to rule in Erik's favor. As the years have gone by, I now understand I was not in the position of persuading God, but He was persuading me. In addition to that truth, I've also realized it was not the kingdom of heaven I was bombarding, but the kingdom of the liar.

Day 18 proved to be a significant one as the neurologist came to brief us. The first comments were very encouraging. "It looks like this boy may live," she said. "However, we need to begin to think about long-term coma care." She continued, "He will never open his eyes, move his fingers or hands. He will never walk again and never speak. What we have now is medically all we can ever hope to have."

I went into prayer after the report, calling God's court in session, I began to battle the new facts of the doctor's prognosis. In prayer I said, "Father, the report says Erik will never open his eyes. I ask that he does open his eyes. The report says Erik will never move his hands and arms, but I ask that he does move his hands and arms. The report says Erik will never walk again, but I ask that he does walk again. The report says Erik will never speak, but I ask that he does speak again. The report says Erik will never wake up, but I ask that he does wake up.

As I was praying, choosing the report of the Lord over the fact of modern medicine, I was suddenly in the courtroom of God. This time I was standing up front, next to the Judge's bench. Jesus was standing beside me, to my left. The pureness of the light was enveloping, yet I could see the prayer I had just prayed lying on the desktop of the Judge. It was similar to:

MEDICAL REPORT	PRAYER PETITION
Never Open Eyes	Will Open Eyes
Never Move Hands/Arms	Will Move Hands/Arms
Never Walk	Will Walk
Never Speak	Will Speak
Never Wake Up	Will Wake Up

The words of the petition were written in red, probably to emphasize to me Jesus' blood had covered these requests all the way back on Calvary. Seeing the prayer so tangibly lying there was powerful.

From the enveloping light, the Father's voice spoke again. "I have received your petitions, now what is the evidence you present so that I may grant these petitions?"

I thought for just a moment, turned to Jesus, and asked Him to turn His back to the bench. I reached up, as Jesus was taller than me, and pulled the robe off his shoulders.

I will forever remember that sight. The numerous scars began immediately at the base of His neck running all the way to His lower back. Layers of scarring revealed some of the scars were deeper than others. The complete scarring of His back reminded me of a severe burn.

"Your honor, 1 Peter 2:24 says, "Who his own self bare our sins in his own body on the tree, that we, being dead to sins, should live unto righteousness: by whose stripes ye were healed." I continued, "Are these scars evidence enough for my brother's healing or are these stripes here in vain?"

Once again, I was standing in the place where I began my prayer. I know the boldness present in the courtroom that day was not out of irreverence, but persuasion. It wasn't my wisdom, but God's wisdom. The very opportunity to see those scars is beyond anything I could have ever even considered happening in my life.

On day 30, the neurologist told us Erik's liver was metabolizing the pentobarbital "like candy." The medically induced coma levels were no longer able to keep him in the coma. The doctor said, "Ready or not, here he comes. We don't know for sure what we are going to get." Later that day, I was standing by Erik's bedside and I said to him, "Erik, if you can hear me, squeeze my hand." Of course, we had said those words innumerable times before. Yet, this time he squeezed my hand. I jumped with excitement and went to his nurse. "He squeezed my hand! He squeezed my hand," I exclaimed. "I asked him to and he did!"

The nurse said it was probably just a reflex. "Listen," I said, "we have been here thirty days, through all kinds of bad news and impossible odds. I don't care what it was. It's the first time in thirty days we've gotten anything from him and I'm going to take it.

Erik was coming out of the coma. Very late in the day, he opened his eyes. I don't think he closed them for three days once they were open. There's no telling how long he had tried to open his eyes and wasn't able. In some ways, it got harder when his eyes opened. He seemed scared and his face was relaying to us he knew he was in big trouble. Yet, it was a day of progress and it kept progressing.

Every day, the prayers continued to be lifted to God. I was becoming bolder and bolder and it wasn't my doing, but God was persuading me out of his Word that He is a miracle-working God. I called court into session many times, read many scriptures back to God. It was the hardest and most glorious labor in my life. I went from believing God could do it, to believing God would do it, to believing, based on the scripture I was returning to Him in faith, God had to do it.

The physical therapy team was called in to start working with Erik's body. In time, the doctors began to discuss moving him to a private room out of the neurology ICU and onto the floor. Erik had lost a lot of weight, his face and body very thin. The crushed area of his forehead above his right eye told a major story. He had to be evaluated by a rehabilitation facility and was accepted for in-patient physical therapy.

The day finally came when Erik was able to leave the hospital. He had yet to say a word or take a step. The very purpose of taking him to rehab was to teach him how to live the rest of his life in a wheelchair. With prayer continuing and the scenery changing, the process of rehab was starting. Within a short time, the therapists came to us and said, "We just might get this boy to a walker!"

Nine weeks after the accident, Erik was sitting in a wheelchair in the cafeteria near his room. He was now able to feed himself. I walked into the room and said, "How's the food?" Erik responded, "Needs salt." These were the first words I heard him say. Trying not to have a heart attack or over-react, I just talked a little more 'small talk'. God was still moving.

As progress continued the therapists moved the bar from a walker to a cane. Erik was going home to Dad's house and would continue out-patient rehab. He was a senior in high school with excellent grades and he wanted to graduate with his class. My sister contacted the school and received the work needed to be done for Erik to receive his diploma. From a mortal wound to the brain in March, Erik was going to his high school graduation in a wheelchair in June.

His name was not called in alphabetical order as were the other graduates. He was being saved for the last name to call. As he was wheeled by friends onto the platform, his name was called, "Erik Shane Hall". Two of his friends picked him up from under his arms, and they walked him to the center where he reached out his hand and took his diploma. The atmosphere was so amazing, my young daughter looked to her mother and said, "Mommy, they are worshiping!"

Around a year later, the neurologist wanted to see Erik in her office. It was just a follow up. I picked him up at Dad's home and took him myself. We walked into the room and she looked upon his 6'4" frame and said something like, "You are very tall."

The room was somewhat clinical, with a metal door painted light brown surrounded by opaque glass separating the office from the hallway. We could see shadows of people as they walked by, yet we couldn't hear their conversations clearly, so I knew we had privacy in there as well. The neurologist sat on the corner of a metal desk with a wood laminated top. She asked if it was okay to talk about all that had happened.

We agreed, of course, anxious to see what she would have to say about it. She began, patting herself on the chest, and said to me, "I took a chunk out of this boy's brain and threw it in the trash. The part of his brain that has your name in it." She continued, "The survival of the impact was unexplainable, but the extent of the recovery is beyond explanation as well. When the rest of his brain sends messages to the removed area, it should be like it hits a brick wall," as she patted the wall behind her. "It should leave him in an utter state of confusion."

"If he were in a wheelchair, out his mind, groaning, drooling, unable to speak, it would still be an unexplainable occurrence. Seeing him, walking, talking, and the fact he knows your name, there are just not words enough to describe the impossibility of that!" the doctor said.

She told us Erik's case study was being used in the neurology department of the medical school. "We give all the stats to the students. They examine all the information we had when the accident happened. It is their job to give a prognosis. On the last day of the class we reveal this was an actual patient and he lived," she said.

She went on to say they were taking the faith of the family into more consideration since Erik's case.

A couple years later, I was in the same hospital to visit a mother whose son had a severe head injury from another accident. Her son clinically was not as bad as Erik, yet life and death remained in the balance. I introduced myself to this mother and told her who asked me to visit. She told me, "I know this is really bad, but I've heard about a young man from our county who had a worse injury a couple years ago. They say he literally lost a part of his brain, but he lived. I'm taking comfort and hope from that story." She continued, "Have you ever heard such a thing?"

I looked at this mother and said, "In fact, I have. That young man was my brother. He lived and now he walks and talks. It is no doubt a miracle, and that is what I've come to pray for here as well."

The same neurologist was walking by and said, "Pastor, are you praying with this mother for her son?" "Yes doctor, I am!" I said in reply. She looked at the mother and said, "He has a better chance."

Erik has received disability since the accident. His ability to concentrate is not what he would need to have a career or even hold down a job. He briefly married, but it was a bit much to endure. His son, born out of that relationship, is now grown, with children of his own. Erik is a grandfather! Medically, he battles some weight issues because his brain doesn't tell him when he is full.

Erik serves as an usher at church when needed. He helps in the yard at home. Nearly ten years ago, he helped us carry our father to his grave. Life has continued.

As for me, I have only one other time experienced stepping into the courtroom of God. On that occasion, I was asked what damages I would like to regain. After pondering the question, I answered, "I ask for at least ten thousand souls be saved because of this miracle." God, through opportunities in mission fields and at home, has surpassed my request, and for that, I give him glory.

Sometimes we forget to remember what a miracle Erik is, as he talks…and talks. A couple years ago, Erik fell down some stairs at Mom's house and broke an elbow. Upon arriving at the emergency room, the doctors scanned him from head to toe, just to make sure there were no other injuries. A doctor came into his room, shaking a scan at my mother. It was the scan of his head. "You've got a story to tell me," he said. "What I see in this scan does not measure up to this man sitting here talking to me." May we give praise to the Judge who sits justly behind the bench in the courtroom of God.

It is somewhat difficult in these days to relate the shock and pain this accident brought into our lives. It was like a flood. Yes, the enemy brought accusation into our minds, and some came out of our mouths, as we grieved and waited out the saga that had taken us into the "valley of the shadow of death" (Psalm 23:4).

It took me time to gather faith and hope. The liar worked overtime to add to our grief and shock by accusing God, blaming Him for the accident, believing He could have stopped it.

As a pastor for 31 years, I now realize the natural course of things take place in our lives, most always. However, I have stood in five continents, and many nations, proclaiming the power of God's love and God's aggressive desire to show Himself to the nations.

He alone is to be praised and I give Him great honor. I love Him and I know He loves you. Who could have spoken such a Word to a sixteen-year old boy, the son of a plumber, all those years earlier and then have the audacity to bring it to pass?

Let us go from Central Kentucky to one of the most powerful moves I have ever seen God perform among mankind, all because of His love. Now we travel to Africa!

2

In a Faraway Land

In 2010, we were partnering with other organizations who joined Joshua Campaign International to reach out to a remote, northern area of the nation of Ethiopia. Many salvations and healings were taking place. I was there to serve, preaching in some of the ministers' services in the mornings and helping wherever needed in the main crusade services in the evenings. This was a new arena for me, seeing face-to-face the faith of a desperate people as they sought the God of heaven to heal their bodies and minds. Blind eyes had opened, deaf ears began to hear, and it was a remarkable first night, no question.

A father caught my eye. He was tall, his wife was to his left, and his daughter was in front of them. It was the desperation I first noticed. He and his wife seemed so crushed, needing God to do something for them. I shifted to see the daughter. It was hard to tell her age, fourteen, perhaps a little older. Her face was smooth and dark. In America, she would be tall for her age. Something was wrong with her but I couldn't tell what. Stepping to the edge of the platform, I reached for them and could barely touch. They were grateful. I prayed, not knowing the need, and there was no evidence of any change. I couldn't get the father's face out of my mind all night long. It bothered me.

The next morning, I joined other ministers in preaching and teaching the indigenous pastors and leaders. It was wonderful to see the hunger in the hearts of these leaders. They gave great attention and clearly loved the Word of God. For the first time in our ministry, I had to use two translators. One translated from English to the national language, the other from the national language to the regional language. The singers were wonderful, and two other pastors ministered as well. We left there for lunch, where we were joined by the street ministry teams who had gone throughout the area. Their reports were amazing and excitement was building.

More and more people were coming into the area. They came on buses, donkeys, motorcycles, horses and wagons, and on foot. After lunch, we had a short time to rest and prepare for the evening service. We began to hear of those coming from a sixty-kilometer distance. God was up to something big.

It was night two of the crusade in Shambu, Ethiopia. Some of the team had been in the healing tent the night before. They invited me to join them but I wasn't sure that was where I needed to be, not after last night. The father, mother and daughter were still on my mind from the evening before.

On this evening, reaching the platform was more difficult than the night before because the crowd had grown. A powerful Ethiopian minister was preaching, and it was effective. He would preach awhile and then people would begin to scream out, vexed by the devil. Music would kick up while team members carried people to the healing tent, then he would preach some more. As the main part of the service began, I apprehensively walked toward the tent.

As I lowered my head and reached to open the tent flap wider, I looked in and saw a packed crowd. Some were deliverance and prayer warriors from the combined teams, but mostly it was people seeking deliverance or physical healing. Some were crying out loudly, others softly. It was hot and humid inside; the need exceeded the comfortable capacity. One of our team workers joined me by my side, and another positioned just behind me.

There was no time for wondering why some were healed and others were not. No time to let humanity get in our way. It was time to work the works of the kingdom of God! The first lady was sitting on the ground. The translators told me of her physical need, and within minutes, she was made whole.

Hearing a noise behind me, I turned to my left to see where it was coming from. An elderly lady was in the grass so out of herself she was more like an animal than human. She was out of her mind. She was so loud! There were three members of the Ethiopian deliverance team working with her. I was very content to let them.

The next person I saw was the young lady from the night before. Her father was standing behind her with his face still filled with the burden of what his daughter was going through. "They came back!" I thought excitedly. How many miss their miracle just because they didn't come back? The translators spoke for the father, telling me his daughter was out of her right mind. I spoke to her with the help of the translators, and a demonic spirit held her under his influence began to show his grip on her life.

At first, I began to command the spirit to leave, having the translators repeat what I was saying. Then I remembered, the spirits know the languages of the world, so why translate? I looked the young lady in her eyes and then told the devil that I knew he understood me and he would have to leave this girl's life. He had her shrug her shoulders like he did not understand. I spoke, "Do not lie to me devil. I know you can understand me!" I went on in the name and authority of Christ, and the spirit left her within minutes. The father was overjoyed, and his daughter fell into his arms. She was free.

People were crowding all around; there was barely any space to move. Another father, this time with a boy, stepped up and told the translators what was wrong with his son. They conveyed the information to me. His son was ten years old and had been paralyzed in his right arm and leg for three years. I asked the father, "What is it that caused your son to be paralyzed? Was it a sickness or an accident?"

The father said, "Oh no, sir. No, sir, it was no sickness and no accident!" I asked him again to tell me the cause of this paralysis. His words may forever be imprinted on my mind.

"We were resting in the middle of the night, then suddenly my son began to cry out in terror from his room," the father said. We jumped up and ran quickly to his bedside. As we reached him, he cried, "Father, Father, I have heard a voice that said to me, 'I am going to paralyze you!'" The father lowered his head and said, "We knew it was the devil, but what could we do? The devil is stronger than we are."

I asked the father if they were believers in Jesus Christ, the Son of God. He affirmed to me strongly, "Yes, sir, yes, sir, we do believe that Jesus Christ is the Son of God and He is our Savior." I told the father the devil had lied to him and his family and Jesus Christ is so much greater than the devil. In fact, the devil does not have permission by God to paralyze his son.

It took about twenty minutes of quoting scriptures affirming that Jesus has conquered the kingdom of darkness, that Jesus was anointed by God to destroy the works of the devil, and that the devil is a liar.

I spoke to the boy and told him to take a step with his right leg. He said he couldn't do it. I told him again, "In the name of Jesus, who has overcome the devil, take your step." On the second try, the boy deliberately took a step. Within minutes, he was walking with both legs. Then he began swinging his right arm without realizing it. I picked his arm up and showed him it was moving also. He looked at it a moment and then went on his way. He had been healed, not from a disease, not from an injury, but from a lie.

As soon as we finished rejoicing, someone took my left elbow and led me to the elderly lady who was still crying out loudly. She was completely out of control. The three members of the Ethiopian team were standing away from her. Her pupils were completely rolled back in her head; only the whites of her eyes could be seen. Her head was tossing back and forth, her arms flying all around. It was a fearful sight. I leaned down with the translator to say something in her ear when a hand reached out for my elbow. It was one of the deliverance team members. They spoke to me through the translator and said to me, "We have a problem." They relayed the demonic spirits in her said they were more powerful than we were. "The devil is a liar!" I responded.

I turned back toward the woman, and once again, I was pulled away. The team members said, "We have another problem. The devils say they are not coming out!"

I pointed my finger toward them and said, "Never believe a demon. They always say they are stronger, there are more of them, and they will not come out. You must know the devil and his demons are liars, and you should not believe them. In fact, when they say they are not coming out, they are fearful they have to come out. When they say they are stronger, they know they are weaker."

This time, when I turned back to the woman, I got near her ear and said, "Human spirit, come back to yourself. I need to talk to you." After two or three times repeating that message, her pupils rolled back around, and she came into her right mind.

She was an elder to me, so I said to her, "Mother, what has happened to you?"

"I have lost my mind," she responded.

"Mother, how did this happen to you?" I asked.

Her story was unforgettable. "I was washing clothes in the river when my natural eyes met the reflection of my eyes in the water. When they met, I heard a voice saying, "I'm going to take your mind." Then, a demon entered my mind through my eyes. I knew it was the devil, but what could I do? The devil is stronger than I am."

I recognized the same lie believed by the father of the little boy. The enemy was intimidating the people of this region with the lie that whatever the devil wanted to do, he could do. Many of the villages had witch doctors in them, and the people had seen others who were cursed by those evil servants of Satan. They were convinced the devil was stronger than the people, and there was nothing they could do about it. They were bound by a lie because they did not know the truth.

"Mother," I asked, "do you believe in Jesus Christ as the Son of God?"

"Oh yes, sir, yes, sir," she said. "I do believe Jesus Christ is the Son of God."

I led her in a prayer to reconfirm her faith in Christ. Then, speaking of her bondage, I said to her, "Mother, you have believed a lie."

I shared with her the truth that Jesus Christ in her is much more powerful than the devil. The Word of God began to roll out of my spirit concerning who Jesus is, how he has defeated the plan of the devil, and her faith in Jesus was about to set her free. She looked at me and said, "I believe this."

Within moments, she was completely free. Now the truth was deeply imbedded into this wonderful woman. The final step to accomplish was to simply command the demons to go. I got in her ear and told the demons they had lost this battle and now they had to get out of her. In the authority of the Word, I commanded the chief demon to leave and take with him every evil spirit under his authority. Brightness filled her face, and her beautiful brown eyes lit up. We stood her on her feet, now in her right mind. The chains she was brought in were no longer needed. Her family members were crying tears of joy, and the deliverance team members were praising God. It was a beautiful sight and a glorious victory for the kingdom of God on this second night of the crusade.

Just as the mother was about to leave the tent, I asked her one last thing. "Mother, tell me, how long was it you had lost your mind?"

She talked to someone in her family and thought a moment. "Fifteen years," she replied. I was simply blown away. This dear woman was out of her mind for fifteen years because she heard a demonic voice and believed the lie she had been told.

We rested well that night and on the third morning, we met for breakfast and a wonderful kickoff before the teams took off again to serve, some of them boarding buses to take them as far as two hours away to remote villages. Several of us who preach went to the morning services to minister to pastors and leaders.

I was asked to take the first message to the people, and things went well. These people loved the Word of God. What happened after the message was a landmark in my life I will never forget. There was a row of chairs in which the ministers sat during service. In front of the three middle chairs was a small table with a plastic tablecloth and a flower arrangement on it. I sat down in the first of the three chairs, Pastor Benjamin from San Francisco sat in the middle, and my assistant, Mike, was in the third. Music was playing between preaching sessions.

Pastor Benjamin looked at me and asked to change seats since he would be the next speaker. I moved to the middle chair. The music wound down, and Benjamin stepped up to preach. When he did, a Swedish brother who leads Joshua Campaign in

Ethiopia, Per, sat down to my right. Mike sat to my left. I was looking toward Mike when I caught just a glimpse of Per out of the corner of my eye. He had a small package of Swedish breath mints and started shaking a couple of mints out into my right hand.

As I turned my head towards Per, I had a déjà vu moment. The tablecloth, the colorful flowers, and the man's hand shaking something out of a package into my hand: it was all in slow motion for a moment. I turned to my left and said, "Mike, I've been here before."

"What do you mean?" he asked.

"I've seen this moment. It has come back to me!"

"When did you see this?" he asked.

"Mike, it was thirty years ago. I was seventeen years old."

As soon as I had said this, I heard a whispering from the Spirit. He said, "Do you not know if I can show you a minute of your life thirty years in advance, the things you are seeing now and believing for now will also come to pass?"

Jeremiah 29:11 says, "For I know the thoughts that I think toward you, saith the Lord, thoughts of peace, and not of evil, to give you an expected end." This verse came personally alive to me like never before. The Jehovah God who produced thoughts *toward* me was now fulfilling them right in front of my eyes and assured me He wasn't finished.

The crusade became massive, and the team began to work as a well-oiled machine. I spent several more mornings in the pastors' sessions and evenings in the healing tents. The deliverance team had asked me to share with them some of the strategies God taught me over the years.

One night, there was rhythmic chanting from a tower belonging to a different religion. It was purposefully loud in order to intimidate and remind the team, and the people of the area, not everyone was happy about what God was doing. A group of college-aged young adults gathered outside on the hotel grounds to pray against the efforts of the enemy. I decided to go to bed.

The next morning, some of the young adults asked me why I had not joined them in the prayer the night before. I said to them, "Young people, the blind see, the lame walk, the deaf hear, the dumb speak, tumors disappear, and people are set free. All the devil can do is chant. I thought I'd get some sleep."

The crusade crowd grew to around 150,000 people. It was what I imagined it was like to live in the days of Christ. The leaders of the meetings asked if I would like to do a "warm-up" message on Sunday morning. In that request, God gave a great insight to our future. He graced me to preach to more people than I had in all my life to that point.

Our route from Addis Ababa, Ethiopia, was through Istanbul, Turkey, and Chicago, Illinois, and then home to Central Kentucky. Layovers, flight time, security and all the rest of the traveling process, accumulated into a thirty-one-hour journey. I was not well physically, which did not help the exhausting saga. It began to feel like an eternal trip.

In some of my better times during the trip home, I contemplated what I had witnessed over and again among the beautiful people of Ethiopia. The testimonies of blind eyes opening, the lame walking, the deaf hearing, the tens of thousands of salvations would be too many to articulate. Even among those who came from the United States to be on the teams, inner healing was needed and received by several.

In the absence of mental institutions and medicines in these remote areas, there was so much need. Deafness abounded because of untreated ear infections due to a lack of antibiotics. Withered hands and arms were created from untreated wounds. Illness and wounds we would treat from the shelves of our drugstores were life-altering events in this land. The same was true with bound minds and emotions.

In the middle of one of our eternal flights, I was in prayer. Within myself, I said to the Lord, "I am so amazed people could literally be out of their right minds for fifteen years because they heard a voice in their thoughts and believed it." It was shocking to see a ten-year-old boy paralyzed for three years because a voice said to him, "I'm going to paralyze you."

I sensed an answer with a mild rebuke within my spirit. "Why does this amaze you?" the Holy Spirit asked me. "How many marriages do you know back home in trouble because of the thoughts going through people's minds? How many ladies have you prayed with because the sexual abuser of their youth told them they were worthless? How many others do you know who are angry with God, their minds believing God doesn't love them because of the things they've been through?"

The Holy Spirit then took me to this verse: "You are of your father the devil, and the desires of your father you want to do. He was a murderer from the beginning, and does not stand in the truth, because there is no truth in him. When he speaks a lie, he speaks *from his own resources*, for he is a liar and the *father* of it." (John 8:44, NKJV, *emphasis mine*)

Having read this passage of scripture before did not prevent it from coming alive in my spirit. Lies come from the resources of the devil. Beyond this, the Holy

Spirit brought new insight as to why Jesus called the devil the father of lies.

3

The Father of Lies

Jesus called the devil the source of lies. In fact, Jesus refers to the devil as the *father* of lies, *not* the creator of lies. In speaking to the Pharisees in John 8:44, Jesus says, "He is a liar and the father of it."

I had spoken the basic truth that the devil is a liar to the deliverance team, the father of the paralyzed boy, and the mother who had been out of her mind for fifteen years. Yet, the Holy Spirit was showing me I myself did not have the full understanding of this truth and the impact it would have on our daily lives from then to now.

The Spirit went on, "Jesus was not making a gender statement when he referred to the devil as the 'father' of lies. He is speaking of the mode of operation by which the devil operates. When you think about it, you realize a father can birth nothing. All a father can do is issue a seed. In order for the seed of the father to bear any fruit, someone has to receive that seed."

Reproducing children would never happen if the seed of every father fell to the ground, having not been received. However, once received, the seed has the potential to create a new reality. My wife and I have produced two children in the natural, so I do know a little bit about the process. Most women begin to have symptoms of being pregnant well before they start showing the physical signs of pregnancy. Some women have morning sickness. Why they call it that, I do not know as it seems to me morning sickness happens at night and in the afternoon too.

In time, those who have received the seed, begin to show. People who do not even know the woman can tell by the symptoms that she is pregnant. The carrying process stretches the body. New clothes have to be purchased to accommodate the changes. The baby continues to grow and begins to kick. A total life change occurs when that which was seeded comes forth.

According to Jesus, the devil's seed is the lie he has told. When people receive the seed into themselves, they become sick with it – morning, afternoon, and through the night. In time, they begin to show they are carrying the devil's lie. People who don't even know them can see the symptoms: they don't trust anyone, they are angry at the drop of a hat, they can't ever seem to be happy, they go from relationship to relationship. The symptoms are too numerous to list.

As we gain knowledge of the truth of God's Word in every area of our lives, we begin to experience more and more the plan of God for us. Our lives will begin to flow in truths, overcoming the lies Satan and his minions have brought to us. Jesus literally said to the people, "Why do you not understand My speech? Because you are not able to listen to My word," (John 8:43, NKJV). Why weren't they able to listen to what Jesus was saying? Because *someone else* already was speaking to their minds and spirits.

It is in my heart for the simple truths you read in this book to make a profound impact on your life and the lives of many other people whose paths you cross. The enemy has relatively few lies to work with; however, he is an expert at presenting them. He and those under him in his government are constantly looking for emptiness and brokenness to allow the seed of the lie to infiltrate deep within us.

In the same chapter Jesus declared the devil to be the father of a lie, He declared the power of a truth, if you know it. "Then Jesus said to those Jews who believed Him, 'If you abide in My word, you are My disciples indeed. And you shall know the truth, and the truth shall make you free'" (John 8:31-32, NKJV). What truth makes you free? It's the truth you *know*.

Let me put the power of knowing the truth into a different context. What if there were millions of dollars left in an account for you? How exciting and wonderful that would be! What an impact you could make on your life and those around you. However, what if you never *knew* this money was left for you? It would do you no good. Truth itself has no benefit *until it is known*. The first step is for us to allow the truth to be *made known* to us. We then have the choice as to whether or not we will receive the truth. Once we receive this truth, it has the power to liberate us.

There are earthly truths, satanic truths, and truths of God's kingdom. All begin and end with the truth that Jesus Christ is the Son of God, born of a virgin, crucified, buried, resurrected from the dead, and ascended to the Father. I've dealt with many people who believed a lie, so much so it *became* truth to them. Lies evolve into deception.

Jesus connected abiding in His Word with our ability to know *the truth*, not just a truth. "Jesus saith unto him, 'I am *the way*, *the truth*, and *the life*: no man cometh unto the Father, but by me,'" (John 14:6, *emphasis mine*). This is a point of contention with the many religions of the world. Various religious views allow for many roads men can travel and get to God the Father, our Creator. However, there is but *one way, one truth*, and *one life*.

> He who sins is of the devil, for the devil has sinned from the beginning. For this purpose the Son of God was manifested, that He might destroy the works of the devil. (1 John 3:8, NKJV)

Notice this passage states Jesus being manifested was and is enough to destroy the works of the devil. Jesus did not have to shed one drop of blood to destroy the works of the devil. He was manifested to destroy the works of the devil. Jesus came in the authority of the kingdom of heaven, as a man anointed of God, and it showed to everyone who was around his ministry.

> And so it was, when Jesus had ended these sayings, that the people were astonished at His teaching, for He taught them as one having authority, and not as the scribes. (Matthew 7:28-29, NKJV)

The blood shed wasn't for the defeat of the devil, but for the Father. It was brought to the mercy seat of heaven and placed before Him.

> But Christ came as High Priest of the good things to come, with the greater and more perfect tabernacle not made with hands, that is, not of this creation.

Not with the blood of goats and calves, but *with His own blood* He entered the Most Holy Place *once for all*, having obtained eternal redemption.

For if the blood of bulls and goats and the ashes of a heifer, sprinkling the unclean, sanctifies for the purifying of the flesh,

How much more shall the blood of Christ, who through the eternal Spirit offered Himself *without spot to God*, cleanse your conscience from dead works to serve the living God? (Hebrews 9:11-14, NKJV *emphasis mine*)

Walk with me as we take a step-by-step journey into the teachings of Jesus Christ. We will combine our life experiences, and the experiences of others, to reach a destination filled with truths. These truths will be powerful enough to defeat every lie and the liar who weaves them.

4

Taking Thoughts

We know the devil is a liar and he is the father of lies. If the devil is lying to us, then we must explore how he is communicating those lies into our lives. Jesus gave us real insight when he was speaking to the disciples about the cares and needs of life.

> Therefore I say unto you, *Take no thought* for your life, what ye shall eat, or what ye shall drink; nor yet for your body, what ye shall put on. Is not the life more than meat, and the body than raiment?

> Behold the fowls of the air: for they sow not, neither do they reap, nor gather into barns; yet your heavenly Father feedeth them. Are ye not much better than they?

Which of you *by taking thought* can add one cubit unto his stature?

And why *take ye thought* for raiment? Consider the lilies of the field, how they grow; they toil not, neither do they spin:

And yet I say unto you, That even Solomon in all his glory was not arrayed like one of these.

Wherefore, if God so clothe the grass of the field, which today is, and tomorrow is cast into the oven, shall he not much more clothe you, O ye of little faith?

Therefore take no thought, saying, What shall we eat? or, What shall we drink? or, Wherewithal shall we be clothed?

(For after all these things do the Gentiles seek) for your heavenly Father knoweth that ye have need of all these things.

But seek ye first the kingdom of God, and his righteousness; and all these things shall be added unto you.

Take therefore no thought for the morrow: for the morrow shall take thought for the things of itself. Sufficient unto the day is the evil thereof. (Matthew 6:25-34, *emphasis mine*)

As Jesus is speaking in Matthew 6:25-34 to his disciples, He has a precise message He presents to be easily seen and understood. If God, our Father, can and does feed the fowls of the air and He is able to clothe the fields with beauty greater than even King Solomon in all his royal apparel, can we not trust God with the need of our tomorrows? Even knowing this, it is not always so easy for our humanity to accomplish a no-worry mindset about our tomorrows.

There is also a subtle message within the message that applies to our thought life. He tells us to "take" no thought about these things. Jesus does not say, *"Think* no thought about your needs." He says, *"Take* no thought" concerning your needs. The key word follows that statement, "Take no thought, *saying,* 'What shall we eat? What shall we drink? What are we going to wear?'"

How do we "take" thoughts? We take thoughts by what we say. Our words give power to the thoughts going on in our mind. I had a couple in my office years ago who were struggling financially and were really weighed down by the season they were in. Every month, they were worried and stressed, yet they seemed to just make it through the month. I remember the husband saying, "Pastor Hall, I just don't *think* we are going to make it through the month *this* month."

I answered with, "That's what you said last month, and yet you did make it. The same God who kept you from last month to this month will keep you from this month to next month." It was comforting to them for someone to point out God's truth at work. In fact, it became the last month they would just barely make it.

The problem with the mindset they had taken was stress, burden and worry wore on them every day of the season because they voiced the thought, "We are just not going to make it this month." The alternative was to have answered the thought with the truth like this: "It feels like, it looks like, we are not going to make it this month. However, it felt that way and looked that way last month. We know God is going to make a way for us this month as well as He did last month."

If the couple had voiced this truth, it would have changed the weight of stress they were experiencing during the season of struggle. An advanced way of coming through the season would have been to say, "Matthew 6:30-31 says the same God who clothes the fields and feeds the birds of the air has promised to take care of us in our season. While we are not yet seeing the fullness of this, we receive this truth into our lives." This biblical truth could have comforted them through the season of struggle.

There is an abundance of teaching on positive confession. I may be just a little different than some of those teachers because it is not my belief a positive confession must include a statement of denial of the circumstance.

There was quite a humorous experience one Sunday morning upon arrival to church. A lady met me in the lobby area, her eyes watering, and voice that was so scratchy it must have hurt to speak. "What is wrong with you?" I asked.

Her reply was, "Nothing, Pastor, I am the healed of the Lord!" She continued, "Would you pray for my body?"

"Well, if you are already healed of the Lord, what shall I pray about?" was my answer.

In truth, Almighty God is not going to fall off His throne if we come to God and tell Him that we are sick. We are to bring our need to Him. It is my conviction that I can also bring my feelings, my fears, and my emotions to this God, who has promised to move on my behalf. My growing tendency is to be brutally honest with my Heavenly Father concerning my thoughts and feelings. Taking ownership of where we are in life prepares the way for truth to enter and things to begin to change. Once I share my thoughts and feelings with my Heavenly Father, I also begin to speak the truth of God's Word to Him. I accept His Word over my feelings and thoughts.

Have you ever had a day you felt God was a million miles away? One morning, it just came right out of my mouth, "God, this morning, I feel you are a million miles away." I didn't stop there. "Now, Lord, I know your Word promised you are with me and you will not leave me in the middle of my journey. I am asking you to lift this feeling of being alone and let me sense the truth of your Word, you are with me." The feeling God was a million miles away began to lift as I proclaimed the truth he is with me-according to his Word.

> Behold, I am with you and will keep you wherever you go, and will bring you back to this land; for I will not leave you until I have done what I have spoken to you. (Gen. 28:15, NKJV)

This truth God spoke to Jacob reveals to us part of the character of God. He does not leave us in the middle of His work in our lives. He has promised to not only speak over us but to be with us until we have arrived into the prophetic future of our lives. I experienced just that during my first trip to Ethiopia, when God reminded me of the moment He had shown me when I was seventeen years old. Thirty years later, it was reality.

It is easy in our culture to get weighed down with the cares of this life. Peter gave us great insight into how to lighten the weight of our cares.

Casting all your care upon Him, for He cares for you. (1 Peter 5:7, NKJV)

The Greek word for 'care' is *merimna.* It speaks of solicitude or distraction. The word for 'casting' is *epirrhipto,* which means "to throw upon". Finally, when it states that he cares for you, it is another Greek word *melo,* which is "to be of interest to and to be concerned about".

In my simple way of speaking, this passage could have been translated, "Throw upon Him all of your distractions because He is interested and concerned about you."

How are we going to lighten the load of our cares if we are too spiritual to throw them upon our Lord? Sometimes we even get some spiritual pride from carrying a heavy burden. Jesus said his yoke is easy and his burden is light. One of my favorite statements is, "If it ain't light, it ain't right!"

Why and how can Jesus say his yoke is easy and his burden is light? We cannot say this about our yokes or burdens, because we are not Christ. We are everyday people who are carrying the weight of *our* world on *our* shoulders. However, we understand Jesus can say this because He has already pulled more than *His* part and has already carried more than *His* weight through *His* cross, *His* death, *His* resurrection, and *His* ascension to the right hand of the Father. Remember, as Jesus taught the disciples, we are to throw our fears and feelings on Him. In order for us to fight these thoughts and feelings, we must use His words in what we say.

The disciples came to Jesus and asked Him to teach them to pray. In Luke 11, His response is recorded:

> So He said to them, "When you pray, say: Our Father in heaven, Hallowed be Your name. Your kingdom come. Your will be done on earth as it is in heaven. Give us day by day our daily bread. And forgive us our sins, For we also forgive everyone who is indebted to us. And do not lead us into temptation, But deliver us from the evil one." (Luke 11:2-4, NKJV)

Notice Jesus declared, "When you pray, say…" There is such a growing trend of silent prayer and bowing our heads in a moment of silence. However, Jesus gives us the first truth of prayer. Prayer is *saying* something to God. He doesn't say, "When you pray, think…," or, "When you pray, blank…" He says, "When you pray, *say*."

The enemy of our souls, the father of lies, has worked diligently to take away the power of prayer by deceiving people into silence. Let us open our mouths and speak to God about where we are, then express our faith in the truth of his Word. Our life changes when we speak the Word of God in faith, believing.

This great prayer Jesus taught us also included a cry for deliverance. Throughout the New Testament, we are given much information about the tactics of our enemy of which we are to be aware. Even the writings of Paul to the Gentile churches include a great deal of understanding and strategy when it comes to dealing with the devil. Let us first examine the mission statement of Jesus Christ.

5

The Mission of Jesus Christ

The Spirit of the Lord is upon me, because he hath anointed me to preach the gospel to the poor; he hath sent me to heal the brokenhearted, to preach deliverance to the captives, and recovering of sight to the blind, to set at liberty them that are bruised. (Luke 4:18)

Jesus came to this earth as a man on whom the Spirit of the Lord rested. The Spirit was there *because* Jesus was anointed to interact with the people of His day, meeting them in their times of need.

Jesus was anointed to do something. Anointing is always accompanied with purpose. His purpose was to minister completely to the need of fallen mankind. Good news was to be given to the poor. The only good news I can think of a poor man needing is he doesn't have to be poor anymore. That notion applies to both the natural and the spiritual state of man.

Jesus was also sent to heal the brokenhearted. There are two Greek words that, used together, translated to 'brokenhearted' by the King James Version. The first is *suntribo*, meaning "to crush completely or shatter". The second is *kardia*, which is "the heart". Has your heart been crushed or shattered? The truth is Jesus Christ was, and is, anointed to heal your broken heart.

I had encountered a young lady who was so brokenhearted she did not believe God could heal her. Our conversation went nowhere until she agreed to trust me with the story of a life trauma.

Her story went like this: "When I was nine years old, my mother's boyfriend raped me on the kitchen floor of our house. He had a knife to my throat. I was so afraid! As he was raping me, my biological mother stood over us watching. She screamed at me, accusing me of being after "her man". She called me a whore. Pastor, why did God let this happen to me?" she asked as tears streamed down her face.

The lie she believed was God had given permission for this to happen to her. He is God, after all, doesn't everything have to come through him? I tried to tell her God has given everyone the power of choice and she had been sinned against by both her stepfather and her mother.

Imagine the added insult to injury when this girl's mother, who should have had a skillet in her hand, beating the back off the rapist's head, instead blamed her nine-year-old daughter for what was happening!

We were making great progress until I asked the young lady if she had ever done anything wrong. "Oh, Pastor, you don't even want to know all the things I've done wrong," she said.

I asked her, "Why didn't God stop you?" Her answer was she had a choice in her actions. "Your mother's boyfriend, and even your mother, had a choice that day," I replied. "God didn't give permission or approve of their actions either. It was their choice."

While there was still much work to be done, the young lady's heart began to heal in regard to the lie that God allowed this to happen. God did not permit these actions as He does not allow the tragedies happening daily around the world. What God does allow is the will mankind chooses to walk in.

> Every good gift and every perfect gift is from above, and cometh down from the Father of lights, with whom is no variableness, neither shadow of turning. (James 1:17)

We all recognize evil and corrupt things happen every day, all around the world. This powerful verse reveals if it is not a good and perfect gift, it is not from the Father of Lights.

Jesus was also sent to preach deliverance to the captive. The Greek word for 'deliverance' is *aphesis*, meaning "freedom or pardon". Jesus did not just come and set the captive free. He came to preach the truth that freedom and pardon were already granted. Truth will set *you* free.

Another interesting word here is the Greek word for 'captive'. It is *aichmalotos*, which means "a prisoner of war". We are to go to the prisoners of war and declare the truth that our Commander has already defeated the commander of the armies of darkness. Because of this, we now have the right to walk out of our prisons and take our freedom.

Jesus continues to relay his mission by saying He had been sent to preach the "recovering of sight to the blind," (see Luke 4:18). The Greek word He used for 'blind' was *tuphlos*, meaning "opaque as if smoky and physically or mentally blind". Notice again He doesn't simply come and heal the blind, but preaches recovering of sight to the blind. For the blind to be healed, they must receive the truth. Jesus is the one who is able to restore their sight.

The lies of the devil are revealed when truth is spoken, whether that truth is that Jesus has the power and compassion to heal the physically blind, or Jesus' teachings are truth enough to destroy the lies of the devil. Truth must be received in order to recover our sight and power.

> In whom the god of this world hath blinded the minds of them which believe not, lest the light of the glorious gospel of Christ, who is the image of God, should shine unto them. (2 Corinthians 4:4)

Now we understand there is also a spiritual enemy coming alongside our natural circumstances to speak his lies, intentionally, for the purpose of blinding our minds to the truth. The truth is, we are fighting both a natural and a spiritual battle.

Finally, Jesus proclaims He has come "to set at liberty them that are bruised," (see Luke 4:18). The Greek word for 'liberty' is the very same used for 'deliverance' earlier in the verse, which means "freedom or pardon".

A bruise is an outward sign of an inward hurt. When we see someone with a bruise, we don't say to them, "Wow, you have a bruise!" Our first reaction to a bruise is, "What happened to you? Are you okay?" The bruise itself tells us it is the result of something else that happened to this individual.

Is your soul bruised? Are your emotions so tender anything can set you off? Are you skeptical about church because someone you thought was a Christian disappointed you?

Jesus said he came to "set at liberty" those who are bruised. He doesn't say he has come to heal them, but to set them at liberty. You need more than just healing from the bruises others bring into your life. You also need to be set free from the hurt you received from their actions.

I asked God one day in prayer, "How do I not give myself to people? I am a pastor, and people are my life!" Quickly, I heard the Father say to my spirit, "Why do you pastor people? Why did Jesus go to the cross? Go to John 14:31." Since I have not memorized the whole Bible, I turned to John 14:31.

> But that the world may know that I love the Father; and as the Father gave me commandment, even so I do. Arise, let us go hence. (John 14:31)

The backdrop to this scene is the upper room. Judas has already gone, and Jesus tells the remaining disciples it is time to fulfill the purpose and commandment of the Father. These are very important key words, "But that the world may know that *I love the Father*; and as the Father gave me commandment, even so I do." (John 14:31, *emphasis mine*)

Shouldn't Jesus have said, "But that the world may know that I love them?" No, Jesus was not here to convince people He loved them. He was here to do the mission God, his Father, had commissioned him to do.

The Spirit said to me, "The cross was the response of two beings' love." God so loved the world He gave His only begotten Son. However, the Son so loved the Father, He gave His life in obedience to the plan of the Father.

The Spirit went on to say, "Son, you do love people, but it should never be your *motive* of ministry. If it is, you will want to quit when people seem unlovable." Learning this truth lifted a lot of pressure I put on myself when it comes to giving myself to people. This truth was one way God began the healing of this pastor's bruises.

Let us look further into some powerful truth to help us defeat the mindset of a victim we may sometimes hold.

6

Defeating the Victim's Mindset

The truth that the devil is a liar and the father of lies has changed even the way I approach helping people who have been wounded by life. Now, when someone comes to me for scriptural help, I sit down with a pad of paper and ask them if they will tell me their life's story and start with, "When I was a child…" Usually, it takes about an hour for them to cover the highlights and lowlights of their life so far. I listen and write down any lies I hear as they tell their story and speak of the impact other people have had on them.

I hear they are the victim of abandonment, sexual sins, lies and gossip, and even disappointment in other people's inability to help them. However, the Lord's Prayer gives us a simple, but profound truth: *we are not victims, but we have been sinned against.*

In Luke 11:1, one of Jesus' disciples asked him to "teach us to pray". Jesus gives the lesson in Luke 11:2-4 where it reads, "And he said unto them, When ye pray, say, Our Father which art in heaven, Hallowed be thy name. Thy kingdom come. Thy will be done, as in heaven, so in earth. Give us day by day our daily bread. And forgive us our sins; for we also forgive every one that is indebted to us. And lead us not into temptation; but deliver us from evil."

Jesus clearly teaches us we get to forgive those who have sinned against us. Yes, you read it right – we get to forgive those who sin against us. This is far different than saying, "I am a victim of…"

While there is much teaching from this prayer, let us focus on Luke 11:4 where it reads, "And forgive us our sins; for we also forgive every one that is indebted to us." There is a clear connection between our forgiveness to others and our forgiveness from God. In applying this truth to people's lives, we have come up with some important steps in this process of forgiveness. Here again, we see the importance of our words.

Forgiveness begins with admission. First, *admit the sin committed against you.* The fourth verse draws our attention to forgiving everyone who is indebted to us. The truth is, we can't truly forgive a debt, or sin, that we do not admit has been committed against us. *Admit the pain the sin has brought into your life.* Many times, people live for years in pain of the sins committed against them. A few of the ways pain of sin lives on after the action took place include: low self-esteem, fear of further hurts, isolation from others, taking blame or feeling guilt for the sin, and blaming God as the source of sin. Finally, *admit the person, or persons, who sinned against you.* We need to take the courage to admit the exact person or persons, who sinned against us. I have people also confess this statement: "It is not all right what they did to me." I ask them to confess that particular message because people need to understand forgiveness is not saying, "It is okay." It is confessing it is *not* okay, but knowing through God we can be healed of these sins.

Healing continues with release, using our words. Letting go starts with *releasing the sin committed against you.* There is only one person in all the universe to whom we can take our own sins, God. This is the same place we can take the sins of others. *Release the pain the sin has brought into your life.* If you need help with the words, say, "God, I release the guilt, shame, low self-esteem, etc. I took from that sin." So many times, the abuser verbally blames the person they are abusing during the event. This is what happened to the young lady whose mother blamed her for the vicious attack of her mother's boyfriend. When releasing the pain, verbally admit to God the many ways this sin hurt you, physically, emotionally and spiritually.

Release the person or persons who sinned against you. Call them by name; first names are sufficient. Sometimes people will call them by relationship, such as "my friend," "my grandfather," "my mother," and even "myself". Sometimes, people blame themselves for their own choices and sins. In this case, you are one of the people you need to release and forgive. If you do not, you will live under the bondage of condemnation for the rest of your days.

It is very important for us to totally reject the victim's mindset. We have witnessed powerful side effects emotionally and in life when people insist on believing they are a victim.

Under this false identity as the victim, we might believe the original victimizer has power over our life, even from the grave. When we accept the lie that we are a victim, we also seem to attract other victimizers like a magnet. The same hurts keep coming into our lives through a variety of people. I believe we inadvertently empower the enemy to continue to *reinforce* our victim's mindset to keep us bound. A lie you believe can become truth to you.

We need to hear and believe the truth that we do not have to be identified by the worst things that ever happened to us. When we accept this truth, Jesus can heal us from the greatest sins committed against us, and we can begin to receive a new truth of hope and a future!

When we accept the truth that we have been sinned against, suddenly we have been empowered. We know who we can take the sin to and how to release it to God. We haven't ignored it or denied it, but we have admitted God is the rightful judge. We release ourselves to our future and promise in Him.

We must know and accept the Word of God, especially those words telling us of redemption, love, grace and truth. You cannot fight and defeat the father of lies if you do not know the person who is the truth. His name is Jesus!

The Lord's Prayer could have been called the disciple's prayer. It is the teaching Jesus gave in response to their request to be taught how to pray. The statement "Give us day by day our daily bread" makes each ingredient important to us every day.

Daily, we need to remember we are of the earth, but God is of heaven and His name is holy. Not only do we need daily bread, but we need Him to forgive, to send forth our trespasses each day. And yet, Jesus does not give an example that itemizes our sins, just the general statement covering all of our sins or trespasses.

If we have an awesome day and can't pinpoint one trespass against God, I don't think it would hurt us to admit we could have missed something. However, there is no need to live in fear that we have failed to confess a particular sin when we have received and issued forgiveness each day.

While we send forth our trespasses, we also need to forgive other people's sins daily as well. While we admit our trespasses and those of others, we all need to be led away from temptation and delivered from the evil one. We do have earthly battles and circumstances, but let us remember we also have spiritual battles with spiritual enemies behind them.

As we keep learning more about the truth, it may surprise many people to notice the many times the New Testament Church was given simple, but powerful, truths about the strategies and methods of our enemy, the devil. We will also see how we can always defeat him. In this next chapter, let us examine the truth of our victory assured as we discuss ways in which we can wage a good warfare.

7

Waging Good Warfare

Many times, the letters of Paul and the other apostles spoke of the devil and his strategies to the Christians who were in the Gentile churches as well as to individuals, such as Timothy. We begin in Romans:

> Now I beseech you, brethren, mark them which cause divisions and offenses contrary to the doctrine which ye have learned; and avoid them.

> For they that are such serve not our Lord Jesus Christ, but their own belly; and by good words and fair speeches deceive the hearts of the simple.

> For your obedience is come abroad unto all men. I am glad therefore on your behalf; but yet I would have you wise unto that which is good, and simple concerning evil.

And the God of peace shall bruise Satan under
your feet shortly. The grace of our Lord Jesus
Christ be with you. Amen. (Romans 16:17-20)

Here, at the end of Paul's writings to the Christians of
Rome, he literally tells them to mark and avoid those
who cause divisions or disunion and offenses. Those
involved in such things create scandals or stumbling
blocks in the church. To 'mark' means to "take aim at,
spy, to scope them out". Paul explains why: "By good
words and fair speeches deceive the hearts of the
simple." So the reason to mark those who cause
divisions or confusion is to protect the newest and
youngest Christians in the church from being deceived
as they are innocent and unsuspecting.

There is such immaturity in the American church and
society that people would be offended at the pastor for
doing such a thing as marking those who cause
divisions. The average Christian in America is hardly
reading or studying the Word of God personally. This
lends them to quickly yield to human reasoning over
the Word of God. They don't know Paul's teachings
tell us to avoid or shun such persons. Maybe if we
followed the Word of God, then people would not be
so quick to stir up trouble in their church.

Paul compliments the church members as being known
with regard to their obedience. He advises them to be
wise in good things and simple in the things of evil.

This notion is also backward from the thinking in America's society. We condemn or make fun of those who are innocent of evil. They are called naive and are made fun of when they should be honored. We would spare ourselves many temptations if we would protect our innocence when we are younger.

Paul also gives a tremendous promise and encouragement when he says the God of peace will 'bruise', from the Greek *suntribo*, Satan under your feet (not God's feet) shortly. God uses His people to obtain the victory. One of the lessons learned here is when we are obedient to God, we are not under the feet of Satan, but he is under our feet.

The Armor of God

> Paul, an apostle of Jesus Christ by the will of God, to the saints which are at Ephesus, and to the faithful in Christ Jesus:
>
> Grace be to you, and peace, from God our Father, and from the Lord Jesus Christ. (Ephesians 1:1-2)

It's important to understand to whom Paul is writing for this part of our study. He is writing to the "saints which are at Ephesus and to the faithful in Christ Jesus." This is important because certainly, by God's grace and our faith in Christ, we may be listed among the faithful in Christ Jesus to whom Paul is writing.

In his teaching Paul says, "Finally, my brethren, be strong in the Lord, and in the power of his might. Put on the whole armour of God, that ye may be able to stand against the wiles of the devil." (Eph. 6:10-11)

Let us remember that Paul is writing to the saints, to the faithful in Christ Jesus, and he is cautioning them to be strong in the Lord and to be strong in the power of His might, not our power. Paul continues, "Put on the whole armor of God" because we need to make a stand.

Paul doesn't warn us of the sheer power of the devil. It is the "wiles", or the methods of the devil, we must be wise enough and armed enough to have done all to withstand. The weapon of truth is so vital to maturity. Truth is a trait of Jesus Christ and a part of His personhood.

> Jesus saith unto him, I am the way, the truth, and the life: no man cometh unto the Father, but by me. (John 14:6)

Jesus does not declare Himself to know the truth or tell the truth, but that He is the Way, the Truth, the Life, and the only narrow road to the Father.

In society and in the church, people are allergic to truth. As men and women of God, we need to be speakers of truth, as described when we read, "That we should no longer be children, tossed to and fro and carried about with every wind of doctrine, by the trickery of men, in the cunning craftiness of deceitful plotting, but speaking the truth in love, may grow up in all things into Him – Christ," (Ephesians 4:14-15, NKJV).

Being able to discern, apply, and properly give truth is a very vital key to maturity. The enemy of our soul would keep us immature so we cannot or will not digest truth. On the other hand, the practice of speaking truth comes with great responsibility. Paul says, "Speaking the truth in love." Truth without love is brutality; love without truth is hypocrisy.

There are many wonderful writings on these weapons of our warfare. In addition to truth, there is righteousness (which keeps our heart), and the preparation of the gospel of peace. Romans 10:15 says, "And how shall they preach, except they be sent? as it is written, How beautiful are the feet of them that preach the gospel of peace, and bring glad tidings of good things!" It is a great thing for me that Paul says preachers of the gospel have beautiful feet because, in the natural, I sure don't. My wife used to say that she loved me from the top of my head to my ankles.

Paul makes another grand statement: "Above all, taking the shield of faith, wherewith ye shall be able to quench the fiery darts of the wicked," (Ephesians 6:16). I have pondered this statement and asked the question, "Why is the shield of faith above all?" Of course we know, "But without faith, it is impossible to please him: for he that cometh to God must believe that he is, and that he is a rewarder of them that diligently seek him," (Hebrews 11:6).

Every other weapon of our warfare must be received by faith. Salvation itself is received by faith. The statement that it is impossible to please God without faith resonates also in the natural realm. Without faith, it is impossible to please anyone. Who wants to be around people who don't believe in them? Notice also that the apostle Paul is not warning *sinners* of the enemy's warfare and weaponry, he is writing to *the church*.

Beware of the Roaring Lion

In 1 Peter 5:1, the apostle says, "The elders which are among you I exhort, who am also an elder and a witness of the sufferings of Christ, and also a partaker of the glory that shall be revealed." Then in 1 Peter 5:5, he includes the younger believers as well: "Likewise, ye younger, submit yourselves unto the elder. Yea, all of you be subject one to another, and clothed with humility: for God resisteth the proud, and giveth grace to the humble."

So now writing to the elders of the church and to the younger leaders following those elders, Peter gives keys to victorious Christian living in just a few verses.

He admonishes them to be "clothed with humility." Clothes are something we put on and take off. We are able to choose humility as we yield to one another. In 1 Peter 5:6, it reads: "Humble yourselves therefore under the mighty hand of God, that *he may exalt you in due time*" (*emphasis mine*).

We have two positions in the kingdom of God: one is to be humbled and the other is to be exalted. It is our job to humble ourselves. It is God's job to exalt us. If we do his job, He will do ours.

> Casting all your care upon him; for he careth for you. Be sober, be vigilant; because your adversary the devil, as a roaring lion, walketh about, seeking whom he may devour:
>
> Whom resist steadfast in the faith, knowing that the same afflictions are accomplished in your brethren that are in the world. (1 Peter 5:7-9)

We once again see an apostle of God is speaking to the church, here specifically to the elders and those whom they are raising up known as the younger ones. The warning is to be sober and to be vigilant because our adversary, the devil, walks about seeking whom he may devour. However, the devil is limited as we must give him permission to devour us. It is time to recognize his voice and tell him, "No, devil, you may not devour me, my future, my generations, or my tomorrows!"

Let me say one last time that the Bible is not warning sinners about the plans of the devil, but the saints of God, even leaders in the kingdom. Victory is assured to those who know Jesus was manifested to destroy the works of the devil.

Submit to God and Resist the Devil

James, the brother of Jesus, was also thorough in his writings to the church with regard to fighting our spiritual enemy, the devil.

> Ye adulterers and adulteresses, know ye not that the friendship of the world is enmity with God? whosoever therefore will be a friend of the world is the enemy of God.
>
> Do ye think that the scripture saith in vain, The spirit that dwelleth in us lusteth to envy?
>
> But he giveth more grace. Wherefore he saith, God resisteth the proud, but giveth grace unto the humble.
>
> Submit yourselves therefore to God. Resist the devil, and he will flee from you.

Draw nigh to God, and he will draw nigh to you.
Cleanse your hands, ye sinners; and purify your
hearts, ye double minded. (James 4:4-8)

When you see the word 'world' in the Bible, it is
speaking of the society of humans upon the earth.
When you see the word 'earth', it is speaking of
mountains, trees, rivers, and all the things making up
this planet. To be a friend of the worldly system is to
be an enemy of God. No wonder there is such an
awkward tension between this world and the teaching
of the kingdom of God. We are here to affect a change
in the mindsets of the people of the world.

God "resisteth" or opposes those who are proud, but
God gives graciousness to the humble. It takes
humility to submit to God, meaning we obey or be in
subordination. In the kingdom of God, this is a willing
obedience, one that chooses to surrender our human
reasoning to receive God's direction, which He gives
in his Word.

It was late in my teen years when Ronald Reagan was
elected as President of the United States. His wife,
Nancy, was a very active First Lady, and one of her
great initiatives was "Just Say No to Drugs." Here we
are thirty years later, and the drug problem is even more
far-reaching than ever before.

The scripture says, "Submit yourselves therefore to God. Resist the devil, and he will flee from you," (James 4:7). You see, you cannot overcome one power until you yield to a greater power. The reason "Just Say No to Drugs" was unsuccessful is people put forth an effort in their own power to overcome a weapon of the devil.

Once we submit ourselves to God, then we can resist the devil, and he will flee from us. To flee is to "run away, to vanish". We can't just party in the devil's worldly system on one hand and pursue God on the other. However, as we have seen earlier in these writings, Jesus did come to preach deliverance to the captives.

Jesus Christ, the Truth walking among us, the Word made flesh, is more than enough to help us realize the benefits of kingdom living. If we would come to Him and then shake the chains that bind us, we would finally see them drop to the ground.

8

Discovering the Real Battleground

For though we walk in the flesh, we do not war after
the flesh: (For the weapons of our warfare are not
carnal, but mighty through God to the pulling down
of strongholds;) Casting down imaginations, and
every high thing that exalteth itself against the
knowledge of God, and bringing into captivity
every thought to the obedience of Christ. (2 Cor.
10:3-5)

Paul makes it clear that while we are physically living
in the flesh realm, we cannot fight the battle in the flesh
realm. The battle truly lies in the spiritual realm, not in
flesh or even intellectual realms. Our spiritual weapons
through God are mighty to the pulling down of

strongholds. From the Twentieth Century New Testament Bible, let us read this passage again:

> For, though we live an earthly life, we do not wage an earthly war. The weapons for our warfare are not earthly, but, under God, are powerful enough to pull down strongholds. We are engaged in confuting arguments and pulling down every barrier raised against the knowledge of God. We are taking captive every hostile thought, to bring it into submission to the Christ. (2 Cor. 10:3-5)

If we can digest the very first sentence, we suddenly become a much wiser Christian. Doesn't it say it all? "For though we live an earthly life, we do not wage an earthly war." This consideration goes much further than the routine Christian will ever get. Most people live their lives believing what happens, happens and do not regard the spiritual warfare surrounding us all.

Others often express their faith that God is in control, so everything that happens has come from Him for some purpose we may never understand. This passage shows us we do, in fact, fight spiritual enemies. Sounds spooky, doesn't it?

Yet, let us not forget, that we also fight these enemies with spiritual weapons. These weapons are powerful and capable. So what are these weapons capable or powerful enough to do? To the "pulling down" of strongholds.

Let's look at the definition of 'strongholds' from the historic Greek text. The Greek word is *ochuroma*, meaning "to fortify with the idea of holding safely, a castle, figuratively, an argument". It is the intention of our spiritual enemies to build rock-solid arguments against the Word of God. They may come from family, friends, fellow churchgoers, teachers and professors, talk show hosts, or from the very thoughts of our own minds. Yes, the spiritual enemies we fight will be masked with human faces.

Dr. Clarence Walker states, "A stronghold is a forceful, stubborn argument, rationale, opinion, idea, and/or philosophy that is formed and resistant to the knowledge of Jesus Christ." Strongholds do two things: first, they keep people from the knowledge of God, resulting in ignorance; and second, they prevent people from obeying the truth, resulting in rebellion.

Today, one of the greatest challenges in helping people is bringing down human reasoning arising to challenge the Word of God. Several years ago, there was a man who attended our church who asked if he could come and talk with me. I set a time, and he came into my office. The man said something like, "Now, Pastor, I want you to know that, in addition to my wife, I also have a girlfriend."

"You have what?" I asked.

"Wait a minute, Pastor. I have prayed about this, and God told me that it is all right with Him. You see, my girlfriend makes me happy, and God wants me to be happy."

"You have lost your mind!" I exclaimed. "God is more interested in you being holy than you being happy, and it would be a bonus if you were happy being holy."

If it is obviously opposite to the Word of God, it did not come from God. Spiritual enemies are whispering into our ears, either from the voices of human beings, justifying their reasoning, or from demonically inspired thoughts. We cannot act as if something like this could only happen to someone else.

Many great outward battles are symptoms of the inward battles going on in the minds of individuals. This is a true illustration of how easily our own minds can be deceived. It doesn't happen overnight, but it could happen to any of us if we forget to cast down the strongholds of life. We have many examples from life of people who need to humble themselves before God. While we have little influence to encourage people to do this, we can certainly make that decision for ourselves.

"Pulling down" is the demolition or extinction of strongholds. This does not sound like God intends for us to have to put up with personal or generational strongholds for the rest of our lives. We will be able to destroy the fortifications the enemy has assembled, even if they have been in our families for centuries.

In 2012, the Lord gave me a little insight into four weapons that the enemy uses in a progressive manner to keep us from living a victorious Christian life in this world. I call them the Four Big Guns of the devil. They are deception, temptation, accusation and intimidation.

9

Deception
The Foundation of Bondage

For many deceivers are entered into the world,
who confess not that Jesus Christ is come in the
flesh. This is a deceiver and an antichrist. (2 John
1:7)

The word 'deceiver' here means an "imposter or a
misleader". There are growing numbers of so-called
Christians who propagate teachings saying Jesus did
not actually come to this earth. They propose the story
of Jesus was just that – a story or parable that was told.

The inspired writer of the books of First, Second, and
Third John was John the Revelator. After spending
much time on the Island of Patmos, John had been
released, now an elder man who was writing to new

generations of Christian believers. Even in that era, he declared that there were many deceivers operating in the spirit of the Antichrist.

We clearly see any voice "who confess not that Jesus Christ is come in the flesh...*is* a deceiver *and* an antichrist" (*emphasis mine*). Once people begin to buy into this deception, it is easy to have them accept Christianity as one of the "many religions of the world."

Make no mistake about it, the force behind such teaching is none other than the devil himself. Let's take a look at Revelation 20:10. "And the devil that deceived them was cast into the lake of fire and brimstone, where the beast and the false prophet are, and shall be tormented day and night for ever and ever."

Notice here the Word does not describe an overpowering, conquering devil, but one that deceived them. It is not the *power* of the devil we are warned about, it is the *methods* of the devil.

> Put on the whole armour of God, that ye may be able to stand against the wiles of the devil. For we wrestle not against flesh and blood, but against principalities, against powers, against the rulers of the darkness of this world, against spiritual wickedness in high places. (Ephesians 6:11-12)

While our enemies look very much human to us, there is a spirit behind them working to deceive as many as possible. I'm not so sure Lucifer just hates mankind so much he wants to destroy them. Perhaps his only interest in us is that God loves us, so the devil wars against what God loves. At any rate, when his judgment comes, the nations of the world are not impressed.

You Mean This is the Man?

How art thou fallen from heaven, O Lucifer, son of the morning! How art thou cut down to the ground, which didst weaken the nations!

For thou hast said in thine heart, I will ascend into heaven, I will exalt my throne above the stars of God: I will sit also upon the mount of the congregation, in the sides of the north:

I will ascend above the heights of the clouds; I will be like the most High.

Yet thou shalt be brought down to hell, to the sides of the pit.

They that see thee shall narrowly look upon thee, and consider thee, saying, Is this the man that made the earth to tremble, that did shake kingdoms;

That made the world as a wilderness, and
destroyed the cities thereof; that opened not the
house of his prisoners? (Isaiah 14:12-17)

The indictment of Lucifer, the "day star" who turned
into Satan the "accuser," could not be more detailed.
His proud heart led him to believe he could wage a
victorious war to establish his own throne above the
other angels and sit in the seat of God. His goal, the
same as those who follow in his deception was to be
like the Most High, his own god. Isaiah 14:16 speaks
of the squinted eyes of man "narrowly" looking upon
him, considering the sight and declaring, "Is this the
man?" You see, no one is saying, "Wow, look at this
beast, this brute of a powerhouse. No wonder we could
not overcome him!" Not at all. They can't understand
how such a snake had so much success. His end is
spent tormented in the lake of fire and brimstone,
forever and ever.

I have some great news for you who are believers in
and receivers of Jesus Christ. We have an eternal devil-
less future ahead of us. I wonder how short of a time it
will take to forget he ever existed. Until then, let us be
wise concerning his deception.

Can the Gospel Be Hidden?

But if our gospel be hid, it is hid to them that
are lost:

> In whom the god of this world hath blinded the
> minds of them which believe not, lest the light
> of the glorious gospel of Christ, who is the
> image of God, should shine unto them. (2 Cor.
> 4:3-4)

The devil has such faith in the "light of this glorious
gospel of Christ" that he knows his only shot is in
blinding the minds of them who do not believe. The
luminosity Satan traded for rebellion has been
succeeded by the Light of the world, Jesus Christ. Let
me show you two other verses revealing some of the
tactics of the enemy in building the foundation of
bondage, which is deception.

These two verses of scripture expose common methods
of the devil's plan to deceive mankind. Remember one
of our weapons against the enemy's lies is for us to
know the strategy or the methods of the devil and his
kingdom.

> Do not be deceived: "Evil company corrupts good
> habits." (1 Corinthians 15:33, NKJV)

I really like this verse in the BBE version as well.

> Do not be tricked by false words: evil company
> does damage to good behavior. (1 Cor. 15:33)

It sounds too simple to put such a thing into the
teaching of the Bible, yet how many people have

damaged their potential, their future, and the promise of God on their lives simply by spending time with the wrong people? The scripture tells us not to be deceived in this. Be cautious of the company you keep. The influence of these people, over time, can begin to numb you toward a downward spiral.

One of my long-time pastor quotes has been, "Christians are like an old car, they start missing before they quit altogether." Years ago, in my very first pastorate, we had a girl who had grown into her middle teen years, and she began to drift from the desire of being in church. This girl was missing a lot more church than ever, and when she was there, she was clearly not connected to what was going on.

Her parents were great folks, and we tried to let them hear our concerns. One night, we got a phone call that this young teen was in an automobile accident. It was a major accident with fatalities, but she was in the back middle of the car and survived, though she still suffered injuries.

It was discovered the older youths in the front seats were drinking and driving way too fast. Our hopes were now maybe the mother would see her daughter was really going the wrong direction and hanging out with the wrong people. The following Sunday, the mother came to me and said, "I am so proud of my daughter because she was the only one of the five in the car who was not drinking or doing any drugs."

My heart sank. This mother had an opportune time to redirect the life of her daughter back toward godly things. Instead, she believed the scenario she was given, and nothing changed. The future brought worsening realities to the family simply because the mother did not want to accept that the evil company her daughter was keeping was damaging her good behavior. We all want to trust our children. However, shouldn't we, most of all, trust the Word of God?

The Inevitability of Reaping

Another powerful verse is found in Galatians 6:7, NKJV. It says, "Do not be deceived, God is not mocked; for whatever a man sows, that he will also reap." This verse, written to congregations of the churches in Galatia, also begins with this stern emphasis: *"Do not be deceived!"*

When I was around twenty years old, I was preaching a revival for a great church and pastor in Ohio. The pastor asked me if I would go to the regional detention center with him to see a church family's son. This young man was the black sheep of the family in that he never really connected to the teachings of God. While the rest of the family were very active and excited about the things of God, this young man quit attending church as soon as he was old enough that his parents felt they could not make him go. The pastor shared with me the circumstances of the young man's crimes. While I won't share those here, it was shocking for a young man to go to such depths.

Upon arrival at the detention center, the pastor asked to see the young man, and it was granted. We were led to a small secured room; it had a small table in the middle and two chairs on each side of it. Another chair was in the corner, where I sat down. The pastor and this longtime youth of his church looked at each other, eyeball to eyeball. After the young man thanked the pastor for coming and engaged in some chitchat, the pastor asked the young man how he was thinking this was going to work out. He answered with something like, "Well, I've never been in real trouble before. I'm thinking they may get me out of here with relatively short time on shock parole."

"Don't be a fool, son," the pastor said. "These are very serious charges."

The boy slammed his two hands on the table, pushing himself to a standing position, and the volume of his voice raised significantly. "It's not fair," he said. "Surely my dad can get the right lawyer and they can get me out here." He continued, "You are here to pray for me. Don't you think God can get me out of this?"

The pastor also slammed his hands on the table and stood up tall, nose-to-nose with this young man. He said, with great expression, "I'll tell you what's not fair, son. There is a woman who will never be the same because of what you did to her, and her husband is dead because of you. Her children have lost a father, and she has lost her husband. You are in Ohio, son. You better pray you don't get the death penalty."

The last time I spoke with that pastor about that boy, I learned the boy had just gotten out of prison, nearly thirty years later. "He's out," the pastor said. "But he is not the same, will never be the same."

This young man, like so many others, believed he could make whatever decisions he wanted, without consequences. You see, "Be not deceived; God is not mocked: for whatsoever a man soweth, that shall he also reap," (Galatians 6:7). So many are sowing and then expecting God to cancel the reaping.

Even the worst of sins can be confessed and washed away in the sinless blood of Jesus Christ! Forgiveness is precious, but it often doesn't cancel the consequences, at least on this side of glory. To conquer this Big Gun of deception, we look to 2 Timothy, where it is written, "Study to shew thyself approved unto God, a workman that needeth not to be ashamed, *rightly* dividing the word of truth!" (2 Timothy 2:15, *emphasis mine*).

To defeat deception we must know the Word in context. Always question to whom and when God was speaking and how it applies to us now. As you read, learn to study the Word in greater detail. Some of our best revelations come from going back to the Greek and Hebrew writings. They were translated long before King James ordered his version.

Through study, you will develop your own thoughts on the scriptures. Be sure to have friends who challenge those thoughts and have been given your permission to question them.

Finally, study the Word in its whole concept. Using just a few words from a whole passage to make a point is insufficient. Partial truth can lead us far away from what God has called us to do. Don't just read what you believe, but believe what you read and follow it. Do this and you will conquer the first Big Gun of the devil, deception.

10

Temptation
The Construction of Bondage

The second Big Gun of the devil is temptation. We must first establish this truth about temptation: the devil did not, does not, and cannot make you do anything. However, he certainly can be your greatest encourager to give in to your desires.

We also know from James 1:13 that God doesn't tempt men with evil. "Let no man say when he is tempted, I am tempted of God: for God cannot be tempted with evil, neither tempteth he any man."

If the devil can't make us do anything evil, and God won't tempt us with evil, where do these temptations come from? "But every man is tempted when he is drawn away of his own lust and enticed," (James 1:14).

This verse emphasizes every human being is subject to temptation when they are drawn away by their own desires and enticed. You cannot be tempted by something you do not want. The desire may not be an action, like doing drugs, drinking alcohol, or engaging in illicit sexual activity. There are so many lonely people in our world, even though they may be surrounded by other people. Loneliness is not necessarily an absence of people around you, but an absence of true relationships with those who are around you.

What you want may be the acceptance of the individual or group who has invited you to party with them. Many people have erred because they just wanted to fit in. On the other hand, you may want and feel you need the high or the numbness to cover the pain in your life. Whatever the root cause, sin lies in wait to find an opportune time to become a temptation.

The Greek word for 'tempted' can also be translated as "tested," and testing comes when we are drawn away, meaning "to drag forth to entice to sin". 'Enticed' means "to entrap," so we are not necessarily captured by it the first time we encounter the temptation. Once we entertain the thought long enough, we are set up for a mess up. When we begin to engage with the action and the people who make up that culture, we are easily taken further into the sin, and the consequences begin to show up.

This Greek word for 'lust' is *epithymia*, defined as "a longing (especially for what is forbidden), a desire". The progression is not quite over even yet. In James 1:15, we read it is when "lust has conceived" that it brings forth sin.

> Then desire when it has conceived gives birth to sin, and sin when it is fully grown brings forth death. (James 1:15, ESV)

The Greek word here for 'conceived' is *sullambano*, "to clasp, seize, arrest or capture". When the lust, or desire, boxes you in, captures you, becomes all you can think about, then it brings forth death.

Pay special attention to these words: "Sin when it is fully grown brings forth death." Sometimes sin starts out with a lot of excitement and fun. Sometimes actions taken with the grandest of intentions to make something better produce strife, confusion and every evil work. If there is confusion, it is not God's work. It would be awesome if we all fully appreciated and understood that God is not the author of confusion. If confusion is produced, either man got in or God got out.

You see, death doesn't have to be physical. Sometimes death falls on a marriage or a partnership, or a church body, or even a dream, purpose, or vision. Sometimes temptation is just seedy, earthly, and plain-out nasty thinking, drawing people to the place of diving into the opposite of what God would have them do.

It is important to be aware of temptation arriving with a compliment or a dream. Temptation can appear in the form of a nice little tune in your heart making you want to dance under the moonlight in complete joy. Yet when yielded to, temptation produces sin; and sin, when it is finished, kills something or somebody (emotionally, physically, or spiritually) graveyard dead.

Faithful to Another

Many anointed people have served under great leaders until they decide it is their time. Jesus said, "He that is faithful in that which is least is faithful also in much: and he that is unjust in the least is unjust also in much," (Luke 16:10). Notice Jesus doesn't end the statement comparing faithful and unfaithful. He compares faithful to unjust. The definition of "unjust" is "treacherous".

On the other hand, Jesus said, "And if ye have not been faithful in that which is another man's, who shall give you that which is your own?" (Luke 16:12).

God asks us to be faithful to what He has given to another man first. This truth gives us room to believe if we have been faithful to another man's ministry, business or family, then God will give us that which is our own.

I once served my pastor's ministry for three months while he was recuperating from an illness. Later in the same year, I went to my first pastorate under the blessing of that pastor. God is faithful and when we are being faithful, we are acting like God. God is faithful, even to our stuff, so we should be faithful to the belongings of another man.

The Wilderness Temptation

In Luke 4, we see the temptation of Jesus Christ in the wilderness. In Kentucky, we live near the Daniel Boone National Forest. Wilderness makes us think of dense growth on steep mountains. In Israel, the wilderness is the southern desert area, the location of the Dead Sea, and the lowest altitude in the world. There are thousands of caves and cave systems in those dry, remote mountains.

> And Jesus being full of the Holy Ghost returned from Jordan, and was led by the Spirit into the wilderness, Being forty days tempted of the devil. And in those days he did eat nothing: and when they were ended, he afterward hungered. (Luke 4:1-2)

When Jesus was most vulnerable, being hungry in his human body, a spiritual attack came alongside of the natural circumstance. "And the devil said unto him, if thou be the Son of God, command this stone that it be made bread," (Luke 4:3). This is a common method of attack by the devil and his minions. He comes alongside natural circumstances and speaks doubt into our minds.

The struggles of everyday life can cause us to question our faith. I knew a family who suffered an untimely, financial burden when their refrigerator broke. Even though it was bound to happen to a twelve year old appliance used by the large family, it still caused them a great deal of stress. The devil came alongside the mechanical breakdown and whispered accusations against God.

Similarly, the devil questioned the integrity of God and the faith of Jesus in the wilderness when he asked, "Why would God lead his own Son into the wilderness? Why would He have his Son be hungry? Why does He not reach out in power and prove something to you?"

Jesus knew, and we must learn, you don't have to prove what you are confident about. Three times the enemy brought Jesus the opportunity to take his calling into his own hands and take over the mission. Instead of turning the stone into bread, Jesus quoted scripture.

"And Jesus answered him, saying, 'It is written, That man shall not live by bread alone, but by every word of God,'" (Luke 4:4). Jesus valued the Word of God greater than his physical hunger.

In Luke 4:5-6, Satan offered Jesus the kingdoms of this world "in a moment of time" and their "glory". In other words, he showed Jesus the gold, the silver, the armies, and the lands of those kingdoms. God had already prophesied the Messiah would someday reign over the nations; so the devil was offering Jesus the power to rule the nations without going through the suffering of the cross. Jesus had the choice to get the same end result his way instead of God's way, but in doing so, He would be found in rebellion against the plan of God. Now this is a temptation.

Yet once again, Jesus quoted scripture: "And Jesus answered and said unto him, 'Get thee behind me, Satan: for it is written, Thou shalt worship the Lord thy God, and him only shalt thou serve,'" (Luke 4:8).

Twice already, Jesus used the old writings of Moses, so now the devil began to quote scripture as well.

And he brought him to Jerusalem, and set him on a pinnacle of the temple, and said unto him, If thou be the Son of God, cast thyself down from hence, For it is written, He shall give his angels charge over thee, to keep thee [Psalm 91:11]. (Luke 4:9-10)

Jesus replied to this misappropriation of scripture in Luke 4:12 by quoting another verse.

And Jesus answering said unto him, "It is said, Thou shalt not tempt the Lord thy God." (Deuteronomy 6:16)

Well, the devil had enough at this point, and he called off the battle as Jesus properly used the written Word of God to ward off his spiritual enemy. "And when the devil had ended all the temptation, he departed from him for a season," (Luke 4:13).

As we remember from our spiritual armor, the Word of God is our sword of the Spirit. Jesus used the Word skillfully, fighting the devil with the same weapons we are told to use.

It is worth pointing out also that Jesus used old covenant promises and the Word because it was all that was available to Him. Yet, the Word of God was enough to send the devil away. Today, we have many more resources with which to sharpen our sword. We have the teachings of Christ through the Gospels. We can employ the instruction of the apostles in the letters to the churches. The prophecies of John the Revelator of the ultimate victory of God's kingdom show us the way. We know of the final judgement of the rebellious

Lucifer. Finally, the precious blood of the spotless Lamb of God was revealed in Revelation 1:5. Truly, we are well equipped to ward off the enemy when he brings the Big Gun of temptation into our lives.

> And they overcame him by the blood of the Lamb, and by the word of their testimony; and they loved not their lives unto the death. (Revelation 12:11)

11

Accusation
The Identity of Bondage

And I heard a loud voice saying in heaven, Now is come salvation, and strength, and the kingdom of our God, and the power of his Christ: for *the accuser* of our brethren *is cast down*, which accused them before our God day and night. (Revelation 12:10, *emphasis mine*)

The third Big Gun of the devil is accusation. The good news from Revelation 20:10 is that the accuser of the brethren, also known as the plaintiff in court, is cast out of heaven. The bad news is given first in Revelation 20:9: "He was cast out into the earth, and his angels were cast out with him." Now the devil and his angels are operating in the world we live in. The accuser is accusing the brethren to one another and to themselves.

The seed of accusation produces condemnation. When the enemy has you locked in the grips of sin and shame, he uses his deception to convince you that you are fine. When you come to Christ, the enemy tries to discourage you from continuing in faith with accusation, tying you to your past.

The only way to prevent the accusations of the enemy from quickly becoming a bondage of condemnation is to learn of the completeness of God's love for us. His is not cheesy love, ignoring all issues and accepting everything and everybody. It is a powerful love, setting sail directly into the storms of our sin and humanity. It is a love that paid a stubborn price to cleanse us, rebirth us, and redefine our present and future!

God's Love in Action

Romans 8:31-39 gives us greater understanding of God's simple yet profound love.

> What shall we then say to these things? If God be for us, *who* can be against us? He that spared not his own Son, but delivered him up *for us all*, how shall He not *with him* also *freely* give us all things? (*emphasis mine*)

I like to say it this way: if God would give us Jesus, how much more would He, along with Christ, also freely give us everything else He has? Once He gave Jesus for us, He will surely, also freely, give us all the other benefits of the kingdom of God.

The word 'freely' derives from the Greek word *charizomai*, meaning "to grant as a favor, gratuitously, in kindness, pardon or rescue". When we ask for financial provision, daily forgiveness, healing, peace, or anything else of God, it is chump change compared to being given the life of Christ.

No Plaintiffs in God's Court

> Who shall lay *any thing* to the charge of God's elect? It is God that justifieth. Who is he that condemneth? It is Christ that died, yea rather, that is risen again, who is even at the right hand of God, who also makes intercession for us! (Romans 8:33-34, *emphasis mine*)

The question is asked, who is going to file any charges to call in as a debt or demand, against God's elect? Who dares to be the plaintiff in God's court? It is God who renders just or innocent. A further question is, who is the one who will condemn? No longer is the answer Satan. Even greater news, the answer is also not Jesus Christ.

Brother and sister, only Christ has died and risen again. Only Christ is seated at the right hand of God himself, making intercession for us. Jesus did not die to condemn us; He died to save us. He is the one who obeyed his Father, even unto the death on the cross. Jesus is not in the ear of God, making accusations against us, so He is not the plaintiff. Jesus is in the ear of God, praying for us.

"My little children, these things write I unto you, that ye sin not. And if any man sin, we have an *advocate* with the Father, Jesus Christ the righteous," (1 John 2:1, *emphasis mine*). The word 'advocate' is our equal to a defense attorney.

Justified

One of the "sounds good, feels good" statements of recent years is a casual definition of the word 'justified'. In church one night, a person told me they had heard the neatest definition of this word. They said looking at the word, we see it in three parts: *just, if,* and *I'd.* Excitedly, they continued, "Me being justified is the same as saying, "Just as if I'd never sinned! Pastor, God looks at my life and pretends like I had never sinned!"

"I think it is much greater than that!" I replied.

You see, if God could simply pretend I never sinned, then God could have:

- *Pretended* to have sent his Son, born of a virgin.

- *Pretended* to have Jesus dwell among us.

- *Pretended* to have Jesus baptized in water.

- *Pretended* to have Jesus tempted in the wilderness.

- *Pretended* to have Jesus arrested, beaten, and scourged.

- *Pretended* to have Jesus condemned by mere men.

- *Pretended* to have Jesus carry his cross as far as he could.

- *Pretended* to have Jesus nailed to the cross.

- *Pretended* to have Jesus hung between heaven and earth.

- *Pretended* to have Jesus declare, "It is finished."

If God could have pretended that I had never sinned, Jesus would have been just a parable. The fact is Jesus was wounded for our transgressions, bruised for our iniquities, surely bore our sorrows. He healed us by his stripes and was raised again from the dead to conquer death. Revelation 1:5, NKJV says, "To Him who loved us and washed us from our sins in His own blood." In Revelation 1:18, NKJV, Jesus said, "I am He who lives, and was dead, and behold, I am alive forevermore. Amen. And I have the keys of Hades and of Death."

This goes far beyond Jesus Christ, God's Son, sitting at the right hand of the Father, saying, "Hey, Dad, give them a break, let's be nice today. Can't we just pretend like they've never sinned?" God most certainly did not pretend as if I'd never sinned.

> Knowing that you were not redeemed with corruptible things, like silver or gold, from your aimless conduct received by tradition from your fathers, but with the precious blood of Christ, as of a lamb without blemish and without spot. (1 Peter 1:18-19, NKJV)

He fully embraced the depravity, the shame, the unthinkable ability of man to murder, rape, dominate, buy and sell one another, make war, and take credit for peace. The foul words of curses, lies, and deceit; the pretense of our goodness; the foolishness of comparing ourselves with one another: all these things fall eternally short of "just-as-if-I'd" never sinned.

In Jesus, the Father found the most innocent of lives and purposed to send him for the guiltiest of lives. "If we say that we have not sinned, we make Him a liar, and His word is not in us," (1 John 1:10, NKJV).

Yes, Jesus Christ is eternally set at the right hand of the Father, and He is praying for us. He does make intercession for and not against us. When He does arise in our defense, it is more likely He says, "Father, look upon my scars, the wounds in my hands, the stripes upon my back. The price has been paid, the blood has been shed. It is finished."

> Then I heard a loud voice saying in heaven, "Now salvation, and strength, and the kingdom of our God, and the power of His Christ have come, for the accuser of our brethren, who accused them before our God day and night, has been cast down. And they overcame him by the blood of the Lamb and by the word of their testimony, and they did not love their lives to the death." (Rev. 12:10-11, NKJV)

This is a great place to remind us the devil does not any longer come before the throne of God to accuse us day and night. He has been cast down and we have been raised up. So many people point to Job and how the devil appeared before God in those days. Yet now "salvation and strength," and "the kingdom of our God," and the "power of His Christ" have come. I must point out the devil was overcome by the blood of the

Lamb and by the Word of our testimony (see Revelation 12:11).

> If it had not been the Lord who was on our side, when men rose up against us: Then they had swallowed us up quick, when their wrath was kindled against us. (Psalm 124:2-3)

How many times can we testify to one another and even to ourselves, "If it had not been the Lord, who was on my side?"

Yes, sometimes it was when men who rose up against us. They sure would have swallowed us up quick in their anger and self-righteousness. Those times are a big part of my testimony.

The Power of Promise

My sixteenth year was a powerful one of prophetic words and encouragement from God. In the introduction, you read the very first of those landmark words that came in that era. However, there was another short, but powerful, responsive Word from God in that time frame.

The church setup was very typical for that day: two sections of pew seating, an aisle down the middle, and one on either side against the walls. An altar space was at the front between the front rows of pews and the platform. If you were looking from the back toward the front, I was standing in front of the first pew on the right-hand side. I had some questions for God: "God, when will the anointing come upon me? God, when will the doors begin to open for this ministry? God, when will there be souls saved?" This prayer was inward and I was burdened.

A young pastor, Steve, came over to me. He touched my forehead and removed his hand, and then the second time, he placed his hand on the top of my head lightly. A strong force came upon me, like it was trying to push me straight down feet first into the floor.

God began to speak through this young pastor. "Anointing? You ask me of anointing? I have anointed you from your mother's womb, says the Lord. Doors? You ask me when the doors will be open? I will open doors no man can close, and I will close doors no man can open, says the Lord. Souls? You ask me of souls? There shall be souls, thousands and thousands of souls."

This landmark experience became a strong force in my journey over the decades. I knew that night I had had a conversation with God. My questions were spoken inwardly, and God spoke verbally back to me through Pastor Steve.

In seasons of discouragement, sometimes at home, sometimes in foreign lands, I would remember the night God answered, in order, those three questions.

At the writing of this book, that event took place thirty-seven years ago. God has since been faithful to His words. I asked for anointing, which is a young man's word for 'utterance'. I wanted to preach, not from my intellect, but from the flow of the Holy Spirit. Years later, I realized even the apostle Paul prayed for such and asked other people to pray it for him.

> And for me, that utterance may be given unto me, that I may open my mouth boldly, to make known the mystery of the gospel, For which I am an ambassador in bonds: that therein I may speak boldly, as I ought to speak. (Ephesians 6:19-20)

If the apostle Paul needed utterance to reveal the Gospel, how much more did I, and still do today? Utterance is still flowing by God's empowering grace.

God has also been faithful in opening doors among nations, revivals in churches and conference-style "teach preaching" (which I call *treaching*), teaching college-level classes, and training new generations of the fivefold ministries.

The final part of God's message was of souls. He said *thousands*. I report God is faithful. Truly He is the Lord of the harvest and very faithful to His Word.

Do not allow the Big Gun of accusation to produce condemnation in your life. I give you this testimony to reflect on the truth that part of overcoming the enemy is by the word of our testimony. Our testimony is not only the great tragedies of our life. May we remember that the wonderful faithfulness of God and his blessings are perhaps the greatest parts of our testimony.

I challenge you to remember the promises God has already fulfilled in your own life. When the enemy whispers or yells into your thoughts that your tomorrows will fail, testify to him and yourself: God was, is, and will always be faithful.

12

Intimidation
To Paralyze with Fear

> Wherefore I put thee in remembrance that thou stir
> up the gift of God, which is in thee by the putting
> on of my hands. For God hath not given us the spirit
> of fear; but of power, and of love, and of a sound
> mind. (2 Timothy 1:6-7)

These powerful and anointed words are spoken from
spiritual father to spiritual son, the apostle Paul to
Pastor Timothy. They bring us to the fourth and final
Big Gun of the devil, intimidation.

God has not given us the spirit of fear. The Greek word
for 'fear' is *deilia*; it is the Strong's Greek Word 1167
– *timidity*. I searched ten Bible versions to see how
they translated this word, and it was largely translated

as one of three English words: fear, timidity, and cowardice. There are some healthy levels of fear, but wherever there is a spirit of fear trying to take hold, there is an intimidator, the devil, behind it.

This is not a fear of going 110 miles per hour down the road, or fear of your girlfriend saying no when you propose to her. These are natural things and worthy of some caution or fear. The intimidator speaks into our spirit, trying to produce a paralyzing fear to stop the furtherance of the kingdom of God. Nearly every effort we've ever made to advance the kingdom of God was met with the enemy's effort to produce fear for the purpose of stopping our efforts.

Overcoming the Spirit of Fear

There are three truths of the Holy Spirit that I want to show you in respect to overcoming the spirit of fear.

The first truth is the Holy Spirit is also known as the Spirit of Promise. The sending of the Holy Spirit was not some knee-jerk reaction of God at the last minute. In fact, it was thousands of years earlier when the prophet Joel spoke of God's plan to send the Holy Spirit:

> And it shall come to pass afterward, that I will
> pour out my spirit upon all flesh; and your sons
> and your daughters shall prophesy, your old men

shall dream dreams, your young men shall see visions: And also upon the servants and upon the handmaids in those days will I pour out my spirit. (Joel 2:28-29)

In Luke 24:29, Jesus clearly tells his disciples He Himself would send the Holy Spirit in response to a promise his Father made. The disciples were to wait in Jerusalem until this promise manifested unto and upon them.

And, behold, I send the promise of my Father upon you: but tarry ye in the city of Jerusalem, until ye be endued with power from on high. (Luke 24:49)

The second truth is the Holy Spirit is also known as the Giver of Power. The disciples were to remain in Jerusalem until they were endued with power. The Greek Word for 'endued' is *enduo* (Strong's Greek 1746) meaning "to invest with clothing". The Holy Spirit would cloak them as a tailor would put a coat on a client and fit it perfectly to him. The result of this new coat is power. This word 'power' is from the Greek word *dunamis* which means "force, miraculous force".

But ye shall receive power, after that the Holy Ghost is come upon you: and ye shall be witnesses unto me both in Jerusalem, and in all Judaea, and in Samaria, and unto the uttermost part of the earth. (Acts 1:8)

The third truth is the Holy Spirit is also the Spirit of Adoption. This gives us the truth God not only saves us, but places us as sons or children of God. There is nothing more assuring as we confront the enemies' spirit of fear than the truth that we are now the children of God.

> For ye have not received the spirit of bondage again to fear; but ye have received the Spirit of adoption, whereby we cry, Abba, Father. The Spirit itself beareth witness with our spirit, that we are the children of God: And if children, then heirs; heirs of God, and joint-heirs with Christ; if so be that we suffer with him, that we may be also glorified together. (Romans 8:15-17)

The enemy cannot defeat us when we understand we have been clothed upon by the very Holy Spirit of God. This Spirit is in us as the very power of the kingdom, power to be witnesses of Jesus Christ around the world.

How multiplied is this truth when we understand we are not simply soldiers of this God, but we are now sons and daughters of Jehovah, the Father of Jesus Christ. We do *not* live under him in the bondage of fear. We did not exchange the bondage of sin for the bondage of fear.

This adoption has brought us around God's table in relationship with this One who has equipped us. We are set free from the spirit of bondage because He has adopted us. He has given us his name. We are now able to approach him as Abba Father.

We do not bow to the spirit of fear when we know we have glory ahead of us as heirs of God. My Abba has already won the victory and therefore, so have I. The spirit of fear can also be described as the spirit of intimidation. I'd like to share a personal experience our family had in this kind of season.

Satan's Effort to Bring Intimidation

Years ago, in late November, a lady came to see me in my church office. When she came in, she said, "There is something I need to tell you."

She proceeded to tell me my life was in danger, an order had been given in the occult to kill me. When I asked if that was all she had to tell me, she was stunned by my ease and readiness to end the meeting.

To her I said, "My life has been in the hands of God for many years. I am just going to continue to trust Him and leave it all in His hands. He is able to protect me and my family." I went home that day but did not share this report. After all, why cast fear on my wife?

On a Monday night the following January, we were in revival at the church. Our friends Jim and Melissa Patillo from Frankfort, Kentucky were singing and preaching in the revival. During the service, someone got my wife's attention and told her we had an urgent call. I noticed the interruption and walked over to see why this person was disrupting the service. My wife had become as white as a sheet.

The man turned to me and said I had to go home immediately. When I pressed for the reason he said, "Your house is on fire! You need to go now!"

In stunned disbelief, I told the church what was happening and called for my mother-in-law and our children to come with us. I asked the church to finish the service even though we had to leave. When we arrived at the entrance of our street, we could see the fire department at our house. The street was blocked off, and a police officer came to my car window. "You can't go down there," he said. "There's a house on fire." When I told him we were the homeowners, he immediately let us through. We could only go so far because of all the fire department personnel at work. It was a cold night, but not impossibly so. We were standing outside, and a neighbor invited my mother-in-law and the kids to come into her house. As church was letting out, a good group of congregation members arrived on our street.

After some time, the fire department declared the fire was out and they walked with me through the house. The scene was unbelievable. The combination of the sight of char with the smell of smoke and water-soaked ashes was surreal. The roof had been burned through, and I could see the stars through the opening. An officer of the fire department brought me into a closet where the fire had started.

He said, "This was a very rare fire in the sense of how it started. Two unusual things happened in order to start this it. First of all, fires usually begin in connection areas like plugs, light switches or junctions. This fire started when a live wire blew in two, touched a two-by-four, and began the burn quickly towards the roof.

This was very rare. When the wire blew, it should have tripped the breaker, cutting off the electricity that started the fire, yet the breaker did not trip. These two things had to happen, back to back, in order for the fire to start. The officer also said it was a very hot fire, and even if we were in the upstairs television room, we may not have known it until it blew the door off the closet.

This very hot fire destroyed the entire second floor of the house. Yet in the closet we had pictures of our children, now in third and fourth grade, from baby times into early elementary school. The pictures were in a plastic convention folder, yet the pictures did not burn or melt. The firemen had no explanation for the pictures' survival of the fire. They still smell like smoke.

We were told we could gather whatever we wanted, which was basically closet items from our room downstairs. The clothes reeked of smoke, dirt and dampness. It wasn't much, but it almost filled the back of our minivan. We pulled out of our street homeless and began to discuss which hotel we would be staying at for the night.

The next morning, I had to go to the store and get basic grooming items and a few other things for the family. Smoke had covered everything the fire did not burn. You don't realize how many things you use on an everyday basis until you have to go get them all at once.

Later, I went by the house to see it in daylight. As I walked up the stairs to the second floor, I sensed something sinister. At the top of the stairs, I could see right into the sky. When I saw my children's beds covered in black soot, my daughter's bed with a doll lying on it forever ruined from the fire, I realized had we been asleep, this event could have been catastrophic.

Then a voice spoke to me, "I could have killed you, and I could have killed your wife, and I could have killed your children."

I was quiet for a moment, and then I answered loudly, "You lying devil. Since when have you shown any mercy? Since when have you restrained yourself from destroying people?"

I continued, "If you could have killed me, my wife, and my children, then we would be dead. The fact is, God protected us. You may have destroyed our stuff, but we are safe and well in the hands of God."

Admittedly, it wasn't so easy to wrap my mind around the materials things either. We were less than a month past Christmas, so my children had lost all their gifts. Being in just third and fourth grade, they mourned their losses, and we needed to let them do so.

This silenced the voice for a season. The intimidator comes to bring fear in such a way as to shut us down with regard to the purpose and plan of God for our lives and those lives He has called us to impact.

It is the devil's plan to steal, kill and destroy. Jesus has a greater plan, and that is to give us life and life more abundantly. He also wants us to pass that gift on to more and more of the people around us.

If the enemy cannot hold you in deception, he will tempt you with things appealing to your flesh. If you overcome current temptations, he will try to condemn you through accusations, tying you to your past. If you overcome the accusations by God's grace, then Satan will do his best to intimidate you and keep you in fear. Intimidation is his last great weapon to keep you from gaining the all-out victory of becoming who God has called you to be.

On the third night in the hotel, in the early morning hours, my wife sat up quickly in the middle of the bed. She was breathing very hard and was clearly shaken. "What is it?" I asked her.

Lela said, "In my sleep, I could see our house burning, and then out of the fire came a woman's face, laughing hysterically."

"Who was it?" I questioned.

Lela called the name of the woman who had come to my office to tell me my life and family were in danger. Lela saw the same woman who said there had been an order given in the occult to kill us.

I then told my wife of the woman coming to my office in late November. All the pieces came together. The woman was sent by the enemy to try and bring fear into our lives. She may have even thought we would decide to run away from our appointment in our city.

We were out of our house for five months and two days. We are still ministering in that same city, but since that time, God has increased the local church and brought more opportunities to spread the Gospel to the poor, as well as preach, and teach pastors around the world.

> For I reckon that the sufferings of this present time
> are not worthy to be compared with the glory
> which shall be revealed in us. (Romans 8:18)

Do not let the devil's Big Gun of intimidation let you forget the weapons we have been given to defeat the enemy.

13

Satan Has No Legal Ground

In late 2007 and into early 2008, the Holy Spirit began to thread through my understanding some compelling revelations. He spoke, "It is human reasoning to think God has given Satan legal ground or rights in the lives of people." The truth is Satan has no legal rights to any soul or to any part of earth.

I know people do things which result in giving place to the devil. The apostle Paul, writing to the church at Ephesus, gave them this instruction, "Neither give place to the devil." (Ephesians 4:27)

This reveals we have the choice whether or not we give the devil a place in our lives. The word, 'place' in this passage, is from the Greek word *topos,* defined as "place, any portion or space marked off, as it were from surrounding space" (Strong's G5117).

We see an example by looking in the parking lots of America. In every lot, you will find handicapped parking. These are portions marked off for the convenience of those who are not able to park far away and walk the distance into the store, church, school, mall, restaurants, etc. Not every spot in a lot is a handicapped parking spot. Only portions of each lot is assigned strictly to the handicapped.

Ephesians 4:27 instructs us not to even give a "place, portion, or space marked off" for the devil to occupy or park on. The emphasis is on what we give to the devil. This verse does not warn us of the sheer ability of Satan to take over a place in our lives. Yet, many people have yielded a portion of their lives to their enemy. Knowingly or unknowingly, they have marked off that portion for the enemy.

A Bad Investment

Another way to get this spiritual truth into our hearts is by understanding our enemy doesn't present the whole truth about what he is up to in our lives. People give place to the devil in the same way someone may invest in a business, only to find out all they were told was fraudulent.

Several years ago, there was much turmoil upon the U.S. economy because of revelations some companies were "baking" their financial reports to make it seem like they were making greater profits than what they really were. Based on these deceptive reports, many people invested in these companies. Perhaps there is no example more famous than the Enron scandal.

Once the investigations ended, it was clear certain Enron executives had deceived many into believing their company was a worthwhile investment. Many people purchased Enron stocks, only to discover the company was not as successful as they appeared. Some of the executives were imprisoned and, unfortunately, one took his life. Notice, it was not the investors who were sent to prison, it was the deceivers.

The devil and his kingdom have no rightful claim on anyone. When people buy into the deceptions his kingdom has produced, it is through misrepresentations, lies, shadows and deception. Most people never even realize they are aligning with demonic principles.

Even when people are drawn into satanic worship and powers, they are deceived by Satan into believing he has conquered Jesus. They may believe he can offer "greater returns" on their investment of service to him than he is really able to pay. I met such a young man many, many years ago.

When I answered the ringing phone, this young and frightened voice said, "Hello, are you a pastor in this town and can you help me?" The caller had dialed our church phone number, which also rang at our house. Our congregation was much too small to warrant a receptionist at the church and this was before cell phones and caller I.D. were common.

I answered his question, "Yes, I am a pastor, and I am willing to try to help you. What can I do for you?" He told me he had just gotten off a bus and was currently at a picnic table at the Salvation Army. He wanted to speak to a pastor who was filled with the Holy Spirit. I agreed to meet him and drove to the Salvation Army. Upon arrival, it was easy to identify this very nervous young man.

He explained to me his mother was an "old-fashioned" Pentecostal preacher in another state. Years before, he had run away from what he called "the rules" and found himself in Florida. There, he had encountered people from the occult and joined them. Now, he was in trouble with them. Somehow, he found out someone who was "under" him had gone to someone who was "over" him and made a pact to have him killed in the weekend activities. The underling was poised for a promotion.

He sat with me at the picnic table very afraid and betrayed by the darkness he was serving. Fortunately,

I had been reading about this group and recognized the name. What I was reading had given specific information regarding how to help free those who were steeply involved in the occult.

We went from the Salvation Army to the church and he repented and asked God to close every door of his life which he had opened to darkness. Long story short, he was set free, forgiven and glowing with a new-found freedom in God. He also had been given a reality check when it came to the lies of the devil and those who served him.

I haven't heard from the young man since, but I will never forget the moment, when on the other end of the phone his mother's strong, country accent cried out, "Is this my boy?"

"Yes, Mama," he replied. "I'm coming home. This preacher in Kentucky has bought me a bus ticket home to you." She wept and praised God for this great miracle. I wept some myself.

The truth is, Satan will never be able to offer eternal positions, power and glory to anyone who serves him. His end is the lake of fire.

> And the devil that deceived them was cast into the lake of fire and brimstone, where the beast and the false prophet are, and shall be tormented day and night forever and ever. (Revelation 20:10)

Notice it was not the devil who overpowered them, or the devil who controlled them, but the devil who deceived them. The end result of people who have been deceived into rejecting Jesus Christ, and his gracious offer of salvation, is also stated: "And whosoever was not found written in the book of life, was cast into the lake of fire," (Revelation 20:15).

Knowing the devil was never given legal ground from God, you don't have to be a spiritual insider to see the devil has influence on the earth and many people have given him authority over their lives. We hardly blink at the news anymore as we so often hear of heinous crimes and unnatural evil taking place. Even as I am writing what God has shown me, the news headlines are screaming of Satan's influence.

> "Twelve-year-old boy beats 17-month-old baby to death with baseball bat because the baby was crying while the boy was trying to watch television."

> "Man murders his girlfriend, then filets parts of her body and cooks it. It is unknown whether he ingested any of the body."

> "Four church fires in Alabama, two Satanists arrested for the fires. One Sunday School room painted with these words, 'Teach children to worship Satan.'"

"Man seen talking to missing hiker in Georgia takes police to her body. Later, he confesses to her murder and is sentenced to life in prison."

"A father in Alabama throws four children, a 4-month-old, 1 year, 2 year, and 3 year old, off 80 foot bridge."

The devil does have influence and authority in the lives of many people. It is also true God did not give Satan authority over mankind in the earth. Satan usurped the authority God gave to man. Satan did not earn it, neither was he awarded it. "The thief does not come except to steal, and to kill, and to destroy" (John 10:10, NKJV).

The Fall of Man

In Genesis 1:6, we begin to examine the creation and fall of man. Here, God first mentions His desire to create man. "And God said, 'Let us make man in our image, after our likeness and let them have dominion over the fish of the sea, and over the fowl of the air, and over the cattle, and over all the earth, and over every creeping thing that creepeth upon the earth.'"

The full pronouncement about this creation shows God not only had a desire for creating man, but He also a purpose in creating man. This new creation did not have to amble about life wondering, "Why are we here?

What is our purpose?" although many people do wonder these questions today. Dominion was given to man by their Creator. God had a right and the authority to give dominion, and man had a God-given right to walk in authority.

Genesis 3:1 states, "Now the serpent was more subtil than any beast of the field which the Lord God had made." The Hebrew word for 'subtil' is *aruwm* and is defined as "cunning (usually in a negative sense)". It is no wonder the devil found a willing partner in the subtil serpent to deceive man into giving up his dominion.

So commonly shared are the traits of the serpent and Satan, that he is called, "that old serpent" in Revelation 12:9 and 20:2. Even though Satan is called a serpent, we have no need to fear him because Jesus gave us authority to tread upon serpents and scorpions. In Luke 10:19, it reads, "Behold, I give unto you power to tread on serpents and scorpions and over all the power of the enemy; and nothing shall by any means hurt you."

In Genesis, 2:16-17, God spoke directly to Adam commanding he never eat from the tree of the knowledge of good and evil. Eve was created after this as a help meet for Adam. No doubt, she had heard of this command through Adam, not God himself. The deceiver focused his attack on Eve and this one command God had given to Adam. Used by the devil, the serpent hisses, "Yea, hath God said, Ye shall not eat of every tree of the garden?" Eve replies, "We may eat of the fruit of the trees of the garden: But of the fruit of the tree which is in the midst of the garden, God hath said, Ye shall not eat of it, neither shall ye touch it, lest ye die," (see Genesis 3:2-3). Eve's reply indicates she resented this command of God because she cynically adds to the command. God had *not* said, "Neither shall ye touch it."

Years ago, I saw a modern-day example of this resentment. Our youth pastor was teaching a series entitled "Spiritual Boot Camp". One of the teenagers cynically told his mother of his experience, "If you leaned back in your chair you were going to hell." This is the same kind of cynicism Eve used. She doesn't trust the heart of God in the command, and she shows it.

So many see the commands of God as restrictive, ridiculous and offensive because they want to do their own thing, not God's thing. They believe God is flippantly giving demands just because He's the boss. Instead they should be seeing the love of God guiding us away from a lesser life and toward a higher life as we honor His guidance.

Society's great challenges today would be nearly, if not totally, eliminated with biblical living. After being given dominion over everything on earth, man resented

God's one Word of restraint. The fruit of the one tree they could not have, became the fruit they wanted more than anything else. It was forbidden fruit and Satan knew it.

Once someone, anyone, even a serpent, came by and agreed with Eve's desire to take of the fruit, she was more than glad to believe the deception of the enemy and take the fruit. Why not? It was a tree bearing food, pleasant to the eyes and to be desired to make one wise.

The lie of the serpent to eat the forbidden fruit in order to be gods themselves reveals the heart of man. Man wants to be like God, without God. Why walk with God, when you can be as God? This is the basis for all rebellion, including Satan's rebellion. He knows this lie well. In fact, he was the first one to be deceived by it.

John the Beloved plainly shows this in the letter of 1 John: "For everything in the world, the cravings of sinful man, the lust of his eyes and the boasting of what he has and does – comes not from the Father but from the world," (1 John 2:16, NIV).

Man was given dominion by God over all the earth, but it wasn't enough. Man wanted to be his own god, calling the shots. By doing so, man lowers his life's impact from eternal to temporal.

The world and its desires pass away, but the man who does the will of God lives forever. (1 John 2:17, NIV)

When we are determined to live after our own authority, we are quickly deceived by the first being who tried such treason: Lucifer, Satan, the devil, that old serpent, whatever you want to call him. He threw away his created purpose with God, and he is more than willing to help you do the same. You won't have to look far to find a lying voice to agree with your desires when you disagree with God.

The Blame Game

Before we leave this story of man's creation and fall, I want you to see one more important issue, the end result of Adam and Eve's disobedience to God. Adam blamed Eve, and Eve blamed the deception of the serpent, yet they all paid a price.

The consequence of Eve's rebellion would be increased pain and sorrow in child bearing. Although it was a part of their dominion on earth to multiply, to increase, and to subdue; now it was going to be much more difficult. The authority of God's blessing had been broken by Eve's desire to be her own god. She was brought under the rulership of her husband and her desire would be for her husband. Eve had dominion over the earth with Adam, but now she would be under Adam's rule.

Adam is rebuked for honoring his wife above God. He listened to her in preference to the Word God spoken directly to him. Adam also wanted to eat of the fruit of the tree but was not ready to openly rebel against God. When Eve approached him with the fruit, he had the best of both worlds in his disobedient mind. If the fruit made him as a god, he got what he wanted. If it didn't, he could blame his wife and God. "And the man said, 'The woman whom thou gavest to be with me, she gave me of the tree, and I did eat,'" (Genesis 3:12). Adam accused God of being at fault for giving this woman to him. Surely God would let Adam off the hook, once He realized it was Eve's fault, not Adam's. Oh, how wrong Adam was.

> And Adam was not the one deceived; it was the woman who was deceived and became a sinner. (1 Timothy 2:14, NIV)

Adam was not deceived, he knew exactly what he was doing and it was high treason. For this, Adam also saw his blessing become his curse. Although he was given dominion over the world, it would no longer bear fruit at his desire. He would now have to sweat, to pull unfruitful things like thistles and weeds from the ground. Only with painful toil would his food come forth. Not only this, but he would not bodily live forever. His body would return to the earth from whence it came (see Genesis 3:17-19).

In Genesis 3:14-15, we read how God dealt first with the serpent. He was the willing partner of the devil in this deception. God curses the serpent more than any other creature. He places him on his belly to crawl and eat dust all the days of his life. The serpent would remember his part in this betrayal as he slithers in the dust from which God took man.

The serpent becomes the enemy of the woman and her offspring. Not only in the physical realm, but God speaks also in the realm of the Spirit to that old serpent when God promises the woman's offspring would crush the head of the serpent. I don't know what promises Satan made to the serpent for his role in this scheme, but I doubt it involved curses, dust and a crushed head. God does not give the serpent or Satan any authority or dominion.

Adam's fall brings a void of authority and dominion on the earth that Satan was more than happy to fill illegally, which is what he wanted in the first place. Satan has never reigned one legal day since the fall of Adam. With lies and deception, the fraudulent kingdom of darkness operates, but it is coming to the day of final judgment.

Until the Ancient of days came, and judgment was given to the saints of the Most High, and the time came that the saints possessed the kingdom. (Daniel 7:22)

Until the final day of judgement, we war against the illegal authority the enemy has taken by receiving the truth of the legal authority God has given to us through Jesus Christ. Satan did not legally acquire man's dominion, he merely filled the empty place left by man's choices.

14

Filling Empty Spaces

When an unclean spirit goes out of a man, he goes through dry places, seeking rest, and finds none. Then he says, "I will return to my house from which I came." And when he comes, he finds it empty, swept, and put in order. Then he goes and takes with him seven other spirits more wicked than himself, and they enter and dwell there; and the last state of that man is worse than the first. So shall it also be with this wicked generation. (Matthew 12:43-45, NKJV)

In this passage, Jesus is teaching the people about deliverance. It begins with Jesus casting a devil out of a man. You will find the beginning of this scene in Matthew 12:22: "Then was brought unto him one possessed with a devil, blind, and dumb: and he healed him, insomuch that the blind and dumb both spake and saw."

The Greek word *daimonizomai* which means "to be exercised by a demon" translates into the word 'possessed'. In other words, the demon inside this man was manifesting. Jesus simply healed the man by casting out the demon; and when the man was healed, he could speak and see.

Numerous times, in crusades around the world, we have witnessed illnesses healed and all symptoms vanish when demons have lost their influence in an individual's life. The people of Jesus' day knew if this man could do such a thing, He must be the Son of David, the promised Messiah.

To squelch the excitement, the Pharisees told the people Jesus had cast out this devil by Beelzebub, the prince of devils. Even the Pharisees could clearly see the devil had been cast out of this man. They then attributed the power to the devil in an effort to discredit Jesus.

Let's visit the idea of demonic possession. It is obvious when devils have truly been cast out of an individual. I personally am very cautious when it comes to using words giving the prognosis of the devil possessing someone. From our experience in hundreds of deliverance sessions, it is clear demons certainly have people under their influence. No doubt, the enemy can live in the soul (mind, will, and emotions) of anyone who will fall into his deception. Those who seek darkness have demonic strongholds in their spirit.

However, legal possession requires purchase. To legitimately possess something requires payment for what is possessed. Neither the devil nor any beings under his authority have ever paid a thin dime for any human being. There is a Spiritual Being who has paid a great price, a matchless price, for every human being. Those who dare to believe will experience the blessings of being purchased by Jesus Christ!

> Forasmuch as ye know that ye were not redeemed with corruptible things, as silver and gold, from your vain conversation received by tradition from your fathers; But with the precious blood of Christ, as of a lamb without blemish and without spot. (1 Peter 1:18-19)

It took the precious blood of Jesus Christ, who was proclaimed the Lamb of God, but we have been purchased. This Lamb was the perfect sacrifice. He was without blemish and without spot. This precious blood is such because it is so rare. No other human being has ever been found without blemish and without spot.

Jesus quickly tore down the false teaching of the Pharisees, who were attributing this powerful deliverance to Beelzebub.

> And Jesus knew their thoughts, and said unto them, every kingdom divided against itself is brought to desolation; and every city or house divided against itself shall not stand: And if Satan cast out Satan, he is divided against himself; how shall then his kingdom stand? (Matthew 12:25-26)

The principle of unity is so vital to every effort, every team, and every kingdom, that even the devil's kingdom cannot stand without it. Could it be the kingdom of darkness, often times, stands in greater unity than the church? God forbid!

Jesus went on to say in Matthew 12:28, "But if I cast out devils by the Spirit of God, then the kingdom of God is come unto you."

Honoring the Holy Ghost

> Wherefore I say unto you, "All manner of sin and blasphemy shall be forgiven unto men: but the blasphemy against the Holy Ghost shall not be forgiven unto men. And whosoever speaketh a word against the Son of man, it shall be forgiven him: but whosoever speaketh against the Holy Ghost, it shall not be forgiven him, neither in this

world, neither in the world to come." (Matthew 12:31-32)

Blasphemy against the Holy Ghost is the vilification, evil speaking, or railing against the Holy Ghost. We must all be very careful to not speak against things we do not understand. Jesus himself says a man can speak against the Son of man and be forgiven, but speaking against the Holy Ghost shall not be forgiven him, not here in this world or in the world to come.

Let us be overly cautious to refrain from speaking against the Holy Ghost. Remember, Jesus is teaching this because the Pharisees were attributing this man's deliverance and freedom to the evil spirit known as Beelzebub when, in fact, the deliverance was the work of the Holy Ghost. Jesus also made very clear that deliverance is the work and manifestation of the kingdom of God.

Jesus gives us the correct information as to what is taking place when an unclean spirit goes out of a man.

> When the unclean spirit is gone out of a man, he walketh through dry places, seeking rest, and findeth none. Then he saith, I will return into my house from whence I came out; and when he is come, he findeth it empty, swept, and garnished.
>
> Then goeth he, and taketh with himself seven other spirits more wicked than himself, and they enter in

and dwell there: and the last state of that man is worse than the first. Even so shall it be also unto this wicked generation. (Matthew 12:43-45)

These verses show us the impact of deliverance. Jesus first speaks of the unclean spirit going out of a man, now walking through dry places and finding no rest. This is surely the work of the kingdom. Something has happened causing this unclean spirit to not be able to stay in this man.

In the writings of Luke, we get more clarification:

When a strong man armed keepeth his palace, his goods are in peace: But when a stronger than he shall come upon him, and overcome him, he taketh from him all his armor wherein he trusted, and divideth his spoils. (Luke 11:21-22)

Now we know the devil could not stay in this man because a stronger Being than he had come. We remember Jesus did not have to shed one drop of blood to defeat the devil. As the Word made flesh, Jesus was already equipped to defeat the devil and his agenda before he died on the cross.

How God anointed Jesus of Nazareth with the Holy Ghost and with power: who went about doing good, and healing all that were oppressed of the devil; for God was with him. (Acts 10:38, NKJV)

The word 'oppressed' here means "to exercise dominion against". Jesus had enough authority as the Word made flesh in his life to defeat Satan and to tear down his strongholds in the lives of those He encountered. Jesus never confronted the devil with His shed blood. He took the blood to the mercy seat of the Father in heaven and left it there.

> For Christ is not entered into the holy places made with hands, which are the figures of the true; but into heaven itself, now to appear in the presence of God for us. (Hebrews 9:24)

Christ did not enter holy places made with hands, but into the holy place in heaven itself. He came to appear in the presence of God for us, not against us.

The greater authority Jesus had in His earthly life was enough to defeat the devil without the shedding of blood. Once Jesus did shed His blood, He did not approach the devil and say, "This is my blood. Leave my people alone!" He approached God with the precious blood of a spotless lamb. This was for the price, or the atonement, of our sins. We are also able to help set people free by walking in the authority, the name, of Jesus Christ.

How an Unclean Spirit Returns

Continuing through Matthew 12:43-45, the unclean spirit returns to "his" house finding it empty, swept, and redecorated. It is clean with new paint, curtains, rugs on the floor and new furnishings. These changes are also the work of the kingdom, but the only problem with this picture is the house is empty.

The Greek word for 'empty' is *scholazo*, meaning "to take a holiday, to be at leisure, by implication, to devote oneself wholly to leisure, or rest". Remember it was earlier declared the evil spirit could not find rest. Now he returned to the house, found it swept, redecorated, and filled with a wonderful, leisurely attitude of vacancy. The original unclean spirit invites seven other unclean spirits into this vacancy, and Jesus proclaims, "The last state of that man is worse than the first," (Matthew 12:45).

There is a Remedy for this Problem

> Be sober, be vigilant; because your adversary the devil, as a roaring lion, walketh about, seeking whom he may devour. (1 Peter 5:8)

The Greek word for 'vigilant' is *gregoreuo*, defined as "to keep awake i.e. watch". To be vigilant and watchful doesn't sound like a great vacation, but it is the way to shut down any opportunity a devil may have to come into your house and take residence.

We must understand the importance of filling empty spaces. I have witnessed countless people who were so empty because of rape, incest, divorce, or the unfaithfulness of a spouse. The great offenses of life open the doors for the enemy to move in without much of a battle to keep him out. We accept so much hurt as just a part of being human.

After a traumatic life event, so many take on a whole new identity for years to come, or even for the rest of their lives. They allow what happened to them to become who they now are, such as the person hurt by the church, the rape victim, or even the perpetrator of such things. Many people blame God for allowing or not stopping the sin that was committed against them.

People say such things as, "God is in control." Common phrases such as this propagate the conclusion that God has given approval for the rapist to rape, the thief to steal, or the liar to destroy. It simply is not true.

> Every good gift and every perfect gift is from above, and cometh down from the Father of lights, with whom is no variableness, neither shadow of turning. (James 1:17)

All the populations of the world should know if it isn't a good gift, if it isn't a perfect gift, then it is not God's gift. While many negative, imperfect things enter our lives, it is not because God gave it permission to be so. Someone else's will has superseded the perfect will of God. Although God did not send those evil, perverted gifts, He will take them from you and heal you if you will surrender them to Him.

When I was sixteen years old, there was a girl about the same age from another church at youth camp. She followed the positive peer pressure of church camp and wound up at the altar one night. I am not sure who started praying with her or for her, but she began to manifest a demonic spirit very loudly and demonstratively. In fact, it took about six men to hold her there for the prayer time. She was a thin person, but unusually strong at the moment.

I was watching from a distance, then closer, and closer again. It was scary in one sense, but also, the Holy Spirit could be sensed. Somehow, I wound up face-to-face with this girl. Several guttural voices were coming out of her. She was wide-eyed and looking for a way out. More truthfully, the demons were looking for a way out.

After some time, she was set free and was sitting before us, calm and in her right mind. We invited her to say a prayer of salvation, inviting Jesus into her life, but she declined. I asked her why, but I wasn't prepared for her answer.

"The demons entertain me," she said. "I received them from the hardest, most guttural rock and roll music I could find. I want them, and I do not want to live without them."

We explained if she left herself empty of Christ, there could be many other demons coming into her house.

"Let them come," was her answer, with attitude.

The last I heard, she was in a mental institution with no hope of being let out.

This was one of the clearest examples I've seen of a house cleaned by the work of the kingdom of God, yet refilled by the enemy because of the temporal entertainment he has to offer. Many people have traded the eternal for the temporal. They are in tune with the here and now, and numb to the price paid for them, unwilling to yield to the kingdom of God.

We have the opportunity to serve whichever kingdom we choose. It is our choice to select the temporal moment or live for the millennial kingdom yet to come. When the days of the kingdom do arrive, we will be so glad God somehow got our attention. We will be delighted we yielded to His invitation and that He allowed us to become the children of God.

Human reasoning says we must ascertain whether someone is open to the Gospel before we set them free with the authority of the kingdom. Yet, how can anyone choose freedom if they are completely bound? Jesus did not implicate the responsibility lies with those engaged in the deliverance ministry, but with the one being swept and garnished after their evil spirit has left.

Jesus said, "Even so shall it be also unto this wicked generation," (Matthew 12:45).

Can you imagine the responsibility upon the generation who saw Jesus face-to-face? Those who witnessed his miracles? Those who ate of bread multiplied? Those who heard of his death and resurrection? Let us not be a part of any wicked generation.

The greater news and truth is there is a kingdom who has a King. His desire is to sweep out the hurts of every house. Further, it is His work to remodel the house and garnish it with the furnishings of the Kingdom of God. It is His desire for every house which has gained sweeping, cleanliness, and received a fresh new beginning to shine as a testimony to His Kingdom and a bright light to the society around us.

> No man, when he hath lighted a candle, covereth it with a vessel, or putteth it under a bed; but setteth it on a candlestick, that they which enter in may see the light. (Luke 8:16)

15

Do You Believe the Gospel?

Every day of our lives, we have the opportunity to be an overcomer. We can overcome by keeping faith in the Word of God. The plan God is unveiling to us is enough to keep us in His grace and mercy until we stand before God and His Christ. The truth is "all have sinned and come short of His glory," (Romans 3:23). Therefore, we all were in the same situation; we needed a sinless substitute to die in our place. Of course, our Substitute's name is Jesus Christ.

Many times, once we have accepted Jesus as our Lord and Savior, we take on the responsibility of earning salvation every day. Not long ago, we had a funeral with some difficult circumstances around it. Someone asked me, "What if the last thing someone does before they die is a sin?"

Can even a believer in Jesus have any hope if the last thing they did in this life was a sin? My answer was, "If sin keeps people out of heaven, no one is going." If all of us have fallen short, how do we know whether or not we are truly saved?

Bottom Line: Do You Believe?

That whoever believes in Him should not perish but have eternal life. For God so loved the world that He gave His only begotten Son, that whoever believes in Him should not perish but have everlasting life.

For God did not send His Son into the world to condemn the world, but that the world through Him might be saved.

He who believes in Him is not condemned; but he who does not believe is condemned already, because he has not believed in the name of the only begotten Son of God.

And this is the condemnation, that the light has come into the world, and men loved darkness rather than light, because their deeds were evil. (John 3:15-19, NKJV)

Let's look at who Jesus was speaking to in this passage. John 3:1 reads, "There was a man of the Pharisees named Nicodemus, a ruler of the Jews." This was a man well trained in the Torah coming to Jesus by night, confessing, "We know that you are a teacher sent by God. No one else could do the works that you do!" (John 3:2, NKJV).

> Jesus answered and said to him, "Most assuredly, I say to you, unless one is born again, he cannot see the kingdom of God." Nicodemus said to Him, "How can a man be born when he is old? Can he enter a second time into his mother's womb and be born?" (John 3:3-4, NKJV)

What a blissful thought, a man having the opportunity to reenter his mother's womb, be reborn, and come forth with the opportunity to start all over again. Who in their right mind wouldn't take the opportunity? "If only I could start over with what I know now." I've heard it a thousand times, and I've said it myself.

We give these verses of salvation to children to memorize as elementary scripture, yet Jesus is speaking to a ruler of the Jews. The simplicity of these words tempts us to overlook their power.

Believe = Not Condemned

> He who believes in Him is not condemned. (John 3:18, NKJV)

Many years of church going implies there are words missing from this verse. Surely, we have to believe and do a laundry list of things so as not to be condemned. The truth is in the exact words of John 3:18, none are missing. In spite of being able to quote the most popular scripture in the Bible, we spend much of our lives living in condemnation. It's not that we don't believe in Jesus, but that we don't believe God could possibly have so much grace for us.

For decades of our lives, we've spent time confessing to God every single unpleasing action we have committed. We may have also spent hours in counseling with our spiritual teachers or preachers. We can be so inept at living worthy that we choose to retreat to a carnal society that convinces us every sin is fine.

If the devil cannot get the world to convince you every sin is fine, he will try to get religious people to condemn you to the point where it seems hopeless to try again.

Perhaps even worse, we may become super-diligent in doing things so pleasing to God, we become certain we have earned the respect of this Holy Being who created us. Self-righteousness may be the greatest obstacle to the simple truth: belief equals not condemned.

I saw the cover of a famous magazine with the picture of a very wealthy man. He gave a total of $1 billion to a variety of charities and causes. The caption on the cover read, "There Is More Than One Way to Get to Heaven."

If good works can get us to heaven, surely God would have had Jesus tell the people of the world to be good and do good things. Would the Father have put his only begotten Son through the brutality of a Roman scourging, then the shame and pain of the crucifixion if good works could bring us into the kingdom of God?

Jesus himself reveals to Nicodemus, a ruler of the Jews, that we must be, and can be, born again. God has sent His only begotten Son that whosoever believes in Him shall not perish. What a challenge, what an opportunity, what a relief!

We Are Bankrupt

One of the greatest of all the challenges of the Gospel is the complete bankruptcy of it. We see this challenge in the choices of individuals throughout the New Testament. Let's capsulize three of these individuals.

The individual commonly known as the "rich young ruler" sought the key to inheriting eternal life. The challenge Jesus set before him was to sell all he had to give to the poor and come and follow Jesus. Jesus said if he chose this option, he would have treasure in heaven (see Luke 18:18-23). When the man heard this, he left Jesus very sorrowful because he was very rich.

Why was this such an impossible route for this man to accept? Isn't treasure in heaven greater than riches on earth? I think the true challenge was for him to give up his earthly identity for the kingdom of God. If he were to sell all he had and give to the poor, and then go and follow Jesus, this man would neither be rich or a ruler. His identity was on the line.

Publicly Desperate

Another individual had to choose to overcome her identity just to approach Jesus in public (see Luke 7:37-39). She is introduced as "a woman in the city, which was a sinner." She didn't have a reputation or identity to protect, indeed her reputation and identity needed rewriting. Equipped with an alabaster box of ointment, she stood behind Jesus in complete humility, weeping. She began to wash Jesus' feet with her tears and wipe them with the hairs of her head. Then, in complete humility, she began to kiss His newly washed feet.

The Pharisee who was hosting Jesus inwardly began to judge Jesus for what was taking place. How could such a miracle worker and a prophet not even have the discernment to know who this ill-reputed woman was? "What manner of woman this is that toucheth him: for she is a sinner," (Luke 7:39). Jesus's answer to the thoughts of this pious man was a parable:

And Jesus answering said unto him, Simon, I have somewhat to say unto thee. And he saith, Master, say on. There was a certain creditor which had two debtors: the one owed five hundred pence, and the other fifty. And when they had nothing to pay, he frankly forgave them both. Tell me therefore, which of them will love him most? Simon answered and said, I suppose that he, to whom he forgave most. And he said unto him, Thou hast rightly judged. (Luke 7:40-43)

We should not intentionally maximize our sins so we may be forgiven of more than others and thereby love our Master more than others. In another scripture, Jesus said, "If ye love me, keep my commandments," (John 14:15).

Jesus is setting Simon up. He is about to reveal our grading systems are skewed. In the reality of it, Simon needed the same love and forgiveness this woman needed. However, she positioned herself in a posture to *receive* forgiveness. She had a far more accurate estimate of her need than Simon had of his own. Simon's judgment of her could not keep her from the Savior's grace for one amazing reason: she knew she was a sinner and humbled herself.

Human beings are very capable of measuring righteousness by comparison. Righteousness by works causes people to boast when the assessment is we have done better than someone else. It also can cause us to hang our head in shame if our comparison shows us lacking.

This woman in the city knew who she was, and she knew who He was. Therefore, it did not matter to her where she was, who was around, or what they thought. It was between her and her Savior.

While Simon the Pharisee was hosting the event, a sinner was worshiping Jesus. True worship is multidirectional. We must humble ourselves as we exalt the One who is worshipped. Simon had a guest; she found a Savior. He could not bring himself to provide common courtesy; she gave all she had. Between Simon and this woman in the city, who loved Jesus the most? Clearly, she did and Jesus readily pointed it out.

And he turned to the woman, and said unto Simon, Seest thou this woman? I entered into thine house, thou gavest me no water for my feet: but she hath washed my feet with tears, and wiped them with the hairs of her head. Thou gavest me no kiss: but this woman since the time I came in hath not ceased to kiss my feet. My head with oil thou didst not anoint: but this woman hath anointed my feet with ointment. Wherefore I say unto thee, Her sins, which are many, are forgiven; *for she loved much*:

but to whom little is forgiven, the same loveth little. (John 7:44-47, *emphasis mine*)

This woman had given herself to every man she could in order to fill that alabaster box. When she found the one man who would give Himself for her, she emptied her box to anoint Him as she gave Him her life.

Would You Flush Your Credentials?

> For we are the circumcision, which worship God in the spirit, and rejoice in Christ Jesus, and have no confidence in the flesh. Though I might also have confidence in the flesh. If any other man thinketh that he hath whereof he might trust in the flesh, I more: Circumcised the eighth day, of the stock of Israel, of the tribe of Benjamin, an Hebrew of the Hebrews; as touching the law, a Pharisee; Concerning zeal, persecuting the church; touching the righteousness which is in the law, blameless. (Philippians 3:3-6)

The apostle Paul was writing to the Philippian church concerning the new circumcision, which is now those who worship God in the spirit and have no confidence in the flesh.

Paul spoke of his Jewish credentials from which he once drew his confidence. He was circumcised on the eighth day, a pure-blood Israel boy, a Hebrew of the

Hebrews. As pertaining to the law, he was a Pharisee Concerning zeal, he adamantly persecuted the church. In regards to the righteousness which is in the law, he was blameless.

Yet this man was stopped on the road to Damascus by Jesus himself to receive a revelation of the Christ. All of his religious achievements did not lead him to Christ. Perhaps what Paul did upon meeting Christ is even more remarkable than all of his earlier achievements. It certainly sets a great example for us.

> But what things were gain to me, those I counted loss for Christ. Yea doubtless, and I count all things but loss for the excellence of the knowledge of Christ Jesus my Lord: for whom I have suffered the loss of all things, and do count them but dung, that I may win Christ. (Philippians 3:7-8)

It is one thing to leave your past behind when your past leaves you with a bad name, a scarred history, and regret from those things you never accomplished. But what if your resumé looked like Paul's? Like we in the western world are blessed to do, Paul's challenge was to flush his credentials and achievements like dung. To win Christ, it was necessary for Paul to lay down those things.

> And be found in him, not having mine own righteousness, which is of the law, but that which

is through the faith of Christ, the righteousness which is of God by faith. (Philippians 3:9)

What? Not having his own righteousness? He stated in Philippians 3:6, "Touching the righteousness of the law, he was blameless." It is not an easy thing to accomplish such a feat.

Paul sacrificed everything for the knowledge of Christ. He counted his former acts of righteousness as dung that "I may win Christ"! Paul's conclusion reveals how extensive his decision was to be totally committed to the revelation of his newfound Savior and to discover the eternal and earthly value of this choice.

The Motive of Paul's Choice

That I may know him, and the power of his resurrection, and the fellowship of his sufferings, being made conformable unto his death; If by any means I might attain unto the resurrection of the dead. (Philippians 3:10)

Paul, having met the resurrected Savior face-to-face, was certain Jesus Christ is the way to eternal life. It was his intention to allow his faith in Christ to bring him to the place where he would attain unto the resurrection of the dead.

The Humility and Purpose of Paul's Choice

Not as though I had already attained, either were already perfect: but I follow after, if that I may apprehend that for which also I am apprehended of Christ Jesus. (Philippians 3:11)

Paul is not only aware of eternal life through Christ, but he recognizes there is a purpose on this earth and in this life for which Christ had apprehended him. Paul pursued Christ so he might understand his specific purpose.

So many times in our church, I have said, "If God just wanted to get you to heaven, He would have killed you the day you were saved." After all, why would God leave us here to be tempted, tried, discouraged, disappointed, and having to live a life of faith? Can you see it? Someone prays the sinner's prayer and then – *boom*, one good knock on the head and "Hello, Jesus!"

The reason we continue here on earth is to be a living, breathing, walking, talking billboard of God's grace and love. We are here to expand the kingdom of God, to present the Gospel to those we come across, saving some.

We are seeking to apprehend the purpose for which He apprehended us. You are filled with kingdom purpose. The final question is this: How do we operate in this mindset?

> Brethren, I count not myself to have apprehended: but this one thing I do, forgetting those things which are behind, and reaching forth unto those things which are before, I press toward the mark for the prize of the high calling of God in Christ Jesus. (Philippians 3:13-14)

Notice that Paul doesn't count himself to have already fully apprehended his purpose. One of the first and most important things we must do is maintain a humble spirit. We have not already reached all God would have us accomplish, nor have we fully become the people He intends for us to become. If we had, we surely would have been ushered into eternity by now.

Paul is taking just one action in Philippians 3:13-14, "I press toward the mark for the prize of the high calling of God in Christ Jesus." He also reveals two tools he uses to press forward.

The first tool is "forgetting those things which are behind," (Philippians 3:13). Remember the things of Paul's past were not all failures. They were great successes. Nevertheless, he had to let go of his accomplishments. Peers who once followed Paul were the ones who now persecuted him.

Yet Paul did persecute the church in his religious past. It took a direct encounter with Jesus on the road to Damascus for Paul to get a true revelation of Christ. The rich young ruler also had a direct encounter with Christ, but was not willing to lose his identity to pursue the kingdom of God. Paul counted all his achievements worthless in comparison to gaining Christ.

The second tool is "reaching forth unto those things which are before," (Philippians 3:13). During the 2016 Olympics, I was watching one of the women's foot races. It appeared a particular runner was about to win one of the dashes when the second place runner dove forward and took the gold by fractions of a second. She stretched forth, no doubt leaving scratches and scrapes on her body, but she was willing to endure pain to win the gold.

This pursuit of God's kingdom and purpose for our lives are worth our efforts to forget those things behind us, whether crushing wounds or mighty victories. It is also worth us reaching toward the future, toward the finish line. The finish line is not simply heaven; it is "the mark of the prize of the high calling of God in Christ Jesus," for your life. Heaven is a great prize, but the greatest prize is to be who He has called you to be.

These are but three examples of many life stories in the scriptures of those who had the opportunity and the choice to believe.

> That if thou shalt confess with thy mouth the Lord Jesus, and shalt believe in thine heart that God hath raised him from the dead, thou shalt be saved. (Romans 10:9)

Believe not = Condemned

> But he who does not believe is condemned already, because he has not believed in the name of the only begotten Son of God. (John 3:17, NKJV)

John 3:17 exemplifies why we must bring the Gospel to every person in our sphere of opportunity. I believe the kingdom of God is searching for believers. Whenever the Gospel is presented, there will be those who mock, scoff, and walk away; and there will be those who receive. You don't have to be a preacher to tell someone about Jesus. Take your faith to work, school, or the marketplace. Tell someone about Jesus at your family reunion.

Don't worry about the kingdom. It does not stop when one does not believe. However, don't lose faith in the power of the good news of the Gospel.

> For whosoever shall call upon the name of the Lord shall be saved. How then shall they call on

him in whom they have not believed? and how shall they believe in him of whom they have not heard? and how shall they hear without a preacher? (Romans 10:13-14)

It is not for us to win everyone we meet, but to present the truth in love to as many as possible. Truth without love is brutality; love without truth is hypocrisy. You don't really love someone if you are not willing to speak the truth to them.

I was embarking on a mission to Ethiopia when I met a lady in the Chicago airport, flying home from her journey. We had a good talk about various things, and inevitably, she asked me where I was going.

When she heard it was Ethiopia, she pursued the conversation by asking the reason for which I was going to this faraway land. I told her of the mission of the Gospel taking me there, and immediately she shrank away from the conversation. She said to me, "Oh, I hope I don't offend you, but I really don't have any religious beliefs. I am just secular."

I assured her I was not offended by her statement, and in fact, it was a statement we hear from time to time throughout the United States. I followed by saying, "I hope I don't offend you, but in Ethiopia, the blind will see, the deaf will hear, the crippled will walk, withered hands will stretch out, tumors will disappear, and souls will rejoice. This will happen only in the name of Jesus Christ. I know this will happen because I have been there before, and this is what happens when people believe in the name of Jesus."

The loudspeaker announced her flight was boarding, and she politely dismissed herself. I do not know if those statements made any change in her beliefs, but I wanted to deposit a seed into her spirit. I also prayed God would send people into her life to water that seed, so a revelation of Christ will be born in her.

Let us sow a seed of the Gospel everywhere we go. This is an amazing Gospel we have in us; it is worth sharing. Years ago, someone told me there are three "SWs" in life: some will, some won't, so what? Do not be paralyzed into inactivity because we are afraid some will not believe. If they never hear the Gospel, they cannot believe. If they hear and don't believe, it is their choice and we have done our job by giving them truth.

To believe is to not be condemned. However, to believe not is to be condemned.

Scriptural Balance for a Great Debate

The inevitable question is, "What then happens if a believer in Jesus commits a sin?"

The Lord's Prayer from Luke 11:4 says, "And forgive us our sins; for we also forgive every one that is indebted to us."

Let me reiterate, Jesus gave us information we need to receive forgiveness and give forgiveness daily. We are also encouraged by 1 John 1:9 to receive forgiveness even after we are saved: "If we confess our sins, he is faithful and just to forgive us our sins, and to cleanse us from all unrighteousness."

The confession of sin to God is not to inform God we have sinned. He already knows. The confession is to inform God we know we have sinned and are not hiding from God. If we confess, then He is faithful and just, both to forgive our sins and to cleanse us from all unrighteousness. I like to say it like this: "Mess up? 'Fess up. Get up!"

> My little children, these things write I unto you, that ye sin not. And if any man sin, we have an advocate with the Father, Jesus Christ the righteous. (1 John 2:1)

The standard is clear: "that ye sin not." Yet, if we do sin, our advocate with the Father remains Jesus Christ. An advocate is an intercessor and can be defined as a defense attorney.

> Who is he that condemneth? It is Christ that died, yea rather, that is risen again, who is even at the

right hand of God, who also maketh intercession for us. (Romans 8:34)

It was Jesus who died and Jesus who rose again. It is Jesus at the right hand of God who makes intercession for us. Someone asked me once if the cross and blood of Jesus were able to cover future sins. My reply was, "I hope so. In relation to the cross, we were all born in the future."

Of course, the blood of Jesus was, and is, enough to wash away our sin!

> And from Jesus Christ, who is the faithful witness, and the first begotten of the dead, and the prince of the kings of the earth. Unto him that loved us, and washed us from our sins in his own blood. (Revelation 1:5)

If we do sin as Christians, we keep believing in the Son of God. We ask and receive forgiveness. We do not live under condemnation, and we daily forgive those who sin against us. However, we need the balance to understand there is a way we can be separated from God and Jesus.

The Reason Jesus Came

> Then said he, Lo, I come to do thy will, O God. He taketh away the first, that he may establish the second. By the which will we are sanctified

through the offering of the body of Jesus Christ once for all. (Hebrews 10:9-10)

Remember that the sacrifice of the life of Jesus Christ was the love of the Father and the Son being demonstrated. God so loved the world, and the Son so loved the Father.

> For God so loved the world that He gave His only begotten Son. (John 3:16, NKJV)

> Arise, let us go from here, that the world may know that I love my Father, I will do what He has commanded me to do. (John 14:31, NKJV)

God so loved the world that He gave his only begotten Son. The Son so loved the Father that He was obedient to go to the cross. We see Jesus was a purpose-driven Savior, but what is the precise purpose of Jesus?

Simply put, it was the will of God that His only begotten Son give His life and shed His sinless blood for the sins of the whole world. Remember, "Unto him that loved us, and washed us from our sins in his own blood," (Revelation 1:5). On our part, we must also remember, "without faith, it is impossible to please God," (Hebrews 11:6). So God does not just apply the shed blood of Christ to everyone, but to those who believe.

We also see from the verses in Hebrews, Jesus took away the sacrifice of animals in order to establish the "offering of the body of Jesus Christ, once for all," Hebrews 10:10). This is why it cannot be of works, self-righteousness, or the worship of any other god to bring us into the kingdom of God.

The Sin of Apostasy = Return to Believe Not

> For it is impossible for those who were once enlightened, and have tasted of the heavenly gift, and were made partakers of the Holy Ghost, And have tasted the good word of God, and the powers of the world to come, If they shall fall away, to renew them again unto repentance; seeing they crucify to themselves the Son of God afresh, and put him to an open shame. (Hebrews 6:4-6)

What I want to show you is the clarity of how any Christian believer could "fall away" from the Word they have heard and the Savior they have received as the atonement for their sins.

This passage is addressed to those who were once enlightened, those who have tasted of the heavenly gift (Jesus Christ), those who were made partakers of the Holy Ghost, and those have tasted the good word of God, and the powers of the world to come.

The potential end of their faith is also spoken of in Hebrews 6:6: "If they shall fall away." The Greek word used here is *parapipto*, meaning "to fall aside, or to apostatize". So the writer is referring to people who were once enlightened *and* fallen away.

It seems clear to me this passage is speaking of those who, for whatever reason, come to the conclusion they no longer believe in Christ, no longer want the heavenly gift, no longer partake of the Holy Ghost, and no longer believe the revealed Word of God. We can consider a couple of reasons someone might come to this place.

Misplaced Faith

I was in my first pastorate for a couple years when a massively powerful and anointed man of God had a very public moral failure. One of the church members asked me this question, "Pastor Hall, would you ever return to the pulpit if you sinned?"

"If?" I asked. "Who do you think that I am? All have sinned and come short of the glory of God!" If sin disqualifies people from ministry, there would be no people in any pulpits.

We must move past the thought that the men and women God uses have to be great people for God to use them. It is a great God who uses mere men and women.

Those of us who are in ministry have a great responsibility to keep ourselves above reproach. Even so, we must also remind ourselves, and others, we are human, and people need to put their faith in Christ, not man.

When we are encouraged or discouraged by the successes and failures of mankind, we are going to live a roller coaster life. Mercy! Our own ups and downs, celebrations and disappointments are hard enough to navigate. Whether it is the courthouse, the church house, the state house, the White House or your house – our devotion to God and faith in God should never depend upon human beings.

Even still, "to whom much is given, much is required," (Luke 12:48). Leaders of churches, cities, countries, and companies, let us do our best in the roles God has given us for surely, we will be required to give an account.

Trials of Life

There hath no temptation taken you but such as is common to man: but God is faithful, who will not suffer you to be tempted above that ye are able; but will with the temptation also make a way to escape, *that ye may be able to bear it.* (1 Corinthians 10:13, *emphasis mine*)

The Word of God promises mankind will experience temptation, but also be given a way of escape. The definition of the Greek word for 'temptation' also includes 'adversity'. These are the trials of life. We have been promised that God has given us the weapons and truths to overcome every life adversity.

Notice Paul does not say that the way of escape will eliminate the season of trial. The word for 'with' is a relational word. I could use it to say. "I have been with my wife for 35 years." In other words, being married to the adversity, the trials and temptations of life, there *is* a way to escape. To find our way of escape, we must be people who know how to hear and do the Word of God in a way that enables us to draw truth, strength, encouragement and stability, even in the worst of times.

> "But why do you call ye me, 'Lord, Lord,' and do not do the things which I say? Whoever comes to me, and hears my sayings, *and does them,* I will show you whom he is like: He is like a man building a house, who dug deep and laid the foundation on the rock. And *when* the flood arose, the stream beat vehemently *to burst upon,* against that house, and *could not shake it*, for it was founded on the rock." (Luke 6:46-48, *emphasis mine*)

The builder of this house had done nothing wrong. In fact, he did everything right. He dug deep, he laid a foundation in the right place, on the rock and yet, the flood came. His house stood because when building the house, the builder knew someday a flood could come into his life. He was so convinced, he spent more time and money in preparing for such an event.

> But he who heard and did nothing is like a man who built a house on the earth without a foundation against which the stream beat vehemently, and immediately it fell; and the ruin of that house was great. (Luke 6:49, NKJV)

Out of this passage, we learn three steps of preparation for the trials of life. We must first go to Jesus. How often we go to a family member, friend or coworker.

Second, we must listen to and understand the sayings of Christ. Reading the Bible is one way to hear the words of Christ. It is also important to sit under pastors and teachers who have been anointed to give you the ability to understand what Christ was teaching. This comes, not only by study, but by revelation and the leading of the Holy Spirit.

Third, in our preparations for the trials of life, we *must do* the words of Christ. We begin to come into maturity when we routinely find ourselves living in obedience to the teachings of Christ. We need to give action to the Word we read and hear throughout our lifetime, doing so consistently and whole-heartedly.

There is a sure enduring power demonstrated in the lives of those who come to Him, hear Him and do the Word He has spoken. These people build. They build churches, they build their families, they build character and longevity. In building, they dig deep. They keep digging and digging, until they find a rock on which to build their foundation. When the flood does come, as it surely will, the builders are not shaken.

The story continues with "And when the flood arose, the stream vehemently beat upon that house," (Luke 6:49). It is just a matter of time for the flood season to come into all our lives. Not if, but when. All manner of human beings experience the flood season.

The other man in the story is the one "who built a house on the earth without a foundation," (Luke 6:49). This man was a builder also. According to Jesus, this man was a hearer, but was not a doer. Having built a house, without a foundation, this man's house fell immediately once the stream beat upon it. As a result, the house was completely destroyed.

My wife and I were young when we met at church camp. We married young so we would keep integrity with our church and God. We've been married now 35 years. During this time, we've had to say good-bye (or "see you later") to all of our grandparents and parents. Lela's brother, and recently even cousins, have gone on their journey to the kingdom of God. We are thankful for the foundation God, through Christ and the Holy Spirit, has helped us stand in difficult days. Yet, we understand we are not the only ones in our generation to have these experiences. We are now the parents and the grandparents.

There are times our battles center around the challenges other people bring into our lives. As pastors, we have been blessed with an exceptional body of Christ to serve for 26 years now. There are still seasons when it is heartbreaking, as we lead real human beings through storms.

You can add the challenges we produce in our own lives by the choices and decisions we have made, and the fruit those decisions bear. I also know life brings adversity quite often through the storms of everyday life. Sickness, tragedy, and grief will enter into all our lives.

I am certain alongside of those events there are voices speaking into our thought lives. Some of those thoughts come from the Holy Spirit. Sometimes they are delivered by other humans. Some of those thoughts are as purely human as you and I.

I am equally persuaded there is a being known as "The Father of Lies" (see John 8:44). He comes alongside of human and earthly events, with the effort to convince us there is no victory here. Jesus Himself bore witness that this being, the devil, is the father of lies.

Yet, when we are sharp, when we are filled with the Word, when we believe beyond what we see, we are destined to overcome the voices speaking lies, and win the victory by knowing and keeping faith in the truth.

> Then said Jesus to those Jews which believed on him, If ye continue in my word, then are ye my disciples indeed; And ye shall know the truth, and the truth shall make you free. (John 8:31-32)

The scriptures make it very clear. You can choose Jesus and come to the Father. If you later apostatize, choosing not to believe in Jesus Christ, there is no other possible way to the Father.

In my experience as a Senior Pastor for 31 years in two different churches, it is rare for someone to stop believing altogether. It is much more common for people to lose faith in themselves (or others) instead of total apostasy, resulting in a true backslidden condition. They may quit church in their disappointment, but not necessarily apostatize.

Many scriptures give us information concerning the enemy of our soul. We are not warned about his brute force or his ability to overpower our lives. We are warned concerning his lies, his wiles, and the methods which he uses to deceive as many people as possible.

Certainly, our current society reflects that people are buying into those lies and believing them as truth.

Unfortunately, there are also multitudes of people in the kingdom of God who also fall as prey into the traps of that luminous being who has turned ever so dark. This is why we must, "Be sober, be vigilant; because your adversary the devil, as a roaring lion, walketh about, seeking whom he may devour," (1 Peter 5:8).

Peter knew what it was to fall into the traps of Satan and was diligent in reminding new generations that we have an enemy who is a *liar*.

About the Author

Thomas Lawton Hall was born in 1963 to Lawton and Brenda Hall. Having preached his first message in a multi-church youth rally in 1972 at nine years old, it has been and remains a priority to someday hear, "Well done thou good and faithful servant."

In October of 1991, he was invited to become the Senior Pastor of The Church of the Living God in Winchester Kentucky. He also serves as a voice to ministers in development at his church as well as through conferences and preaching opportunities in the United States and around the world.

Thomas received his master's degree from Life Christian University in Tampa, Florida.

His life-long vision is to affect a change among the lost, the bound, and all others who are pursuing their God-authored destiny in this world and in the Kingdom yet to come.

9 780998 101385